Konrad Graf

Satori

A Journey To Inner Mastery

First edition

Table of Contents

Introduction

In a world constantly brimming with noise, distractions, and relentless demands, we often lose sight of ourselves, detached from the deeper truths of existence. We run, we strive, and we chase after fleeting goals, hoping that somewhere at the end of the race lies fulfillment, only to discover that the finish line keeps moving. What if the fulfillment we seek isn't waiting at the end of some distant journey but is quietly present in the here and now? What if the key to inner peace and profound understanding lies not in attaining something new but in letting go of what obscures the truth? This is the essence of Satori.

Still, I get it. If „awakening" sounds like a sales pitch from a guy in a poncho peddling crystals, I don't blame you for tuning out. I'd have bolted for the door myself at some point. This isn't about incense or cosmic hugs; it's about ditching the mental junk we lug around, using things you're already halfway doing, like walking off a bad day or skipping the third coffee. Think it's fluff? Next time you're stuck in traffic, cursing the universe, unclench your jaw, look out the window, and let the moment sit. Feel a flicker of calm? That's the start—no robes, no rituals, just a toe in the water.

Satori, in Zen Buddhism, represents a sudden flash of enlightenment, a moment when the fog clears, and we see reality as it truly is. This work is not about prescribing a rigid path to enlightenment or promising an instant transformation. Instead, it's an invitation to embark on a journey of self-discovery, to unravel the layers of illusions, attachments, and narratives that keep us from experiencing the fullness of life.

Although my words may occasionally come across as strong, I want to emphasize that these writings are not intended to judge or assess anyone's character. Rather, these are reflections drawn from both personal experiences and shared challenges. I aim to share the realizations that have profoundly transformed my own life, with the hope that they might serve as a source of guidance for anyone striving for a more harmonious and fulfilling existence.

The inspiration behind these reflections came from the struggles of two friends facing depression. Though their experiences were unique, their challenges mirrored my own. This book is a collection of insights that have profoundly enriched my life. My purpose is to guide you toward an effortless life in harmony with the world. This is a roadmap I wish I'd had during my struggles. Many of the ideas here were inspired by other great thinkers, but this is an attempt at something I feel is missing. It is an attempt to be accurate yet also describe the broad spectrum of the human experience. Learning about the universe often felt like peeling back layers of mystery to grasp deeper truths. However, it is probably impossible to transfer information from one person to another without loss, given that language is a very limited medium. Still, I hope my efforts here help you find a happier, more connected life.

To illustrate how quickly our lens on reality can change, let's consider an everyday example: Everybody knows what coffee does. One moment, you're a sloth, the next, you're Marie Kondo-ing your garage at 7 a.m. It's like legal magic, but less sparkly. Mind-altering substances like alcohol or coffee are commonly found in our culture. These effects are even more noticeable with harder drugs. You just need to ask a raver dancing their soul out in the middle of an industrial warehouse, having the time of their life.

That same person might have been timid and scared out of their mind when they arrived. After all, the event might have been illegal, and they were trespassing on that property right now. Did the industrial, brutalist warehouse change its appearance and become a beautiful jungle loft overlooking an exotic canyon filled with beautiful, astonishing life? The environment did not change, yet our raver seems to be having the time of their life. What changed wasn't the environment but their chemical-induced perception of the environment. If you had a conversation with the same person on the street, you might feel like you are talking to a different person. Their personality changed from a timid and maybe grumpy person into a friendly and open-minded person.

I am not advocating illegal substances or trespassing on property. But it is without question that the chemicals flooding our brains constitute our personality at any given time. Doesn't this also mean that our personality can be changed in an instant if we change the composition of the neurotransmitters and enzymes in our brain? Yet, it seems we have a strong belief about who we are. Why is that? Some people will carry this belief about themselves until the end of their lives, leaving them with not only a monotonous but also a bitter experience of life.

Our personality is the lens through which we experience the world and see reality. If we want to change our experience, we need to change our personality. But if it were so easy to change our personality, then you would not be reading this book. We know we *shouldn't* binge a whole season of a show in one sitting or yell at the printer, but here we are anyway, Netflix on, paper jam rage mode activated. What we are missing, however, is a proper understanding of the tools and how to use them to change our personality and, therefore, our experience.

We are all caught in illusions of this world and how well everybody else must be doing. However, this is simply not true. The majority of people have one or another way of being messed up. No one is cut from a different cloth. Why does it seem some people have such an easy life or seem more resilient than others? They aren't. There are, however, several things they realized along the way, which changed their perception and thereby changed their destiny. Hopefully, this book will give you some insights into this.

Despite what many people want to believe, no one is born exceptional. Sure, for certain activities, you need to be one of the outliers of the genetic lottery, but even then, there are always exceptions to these rules. If we take basketball, for example, we will find that it is almost impossible to be a professional if you are below 1.83 meters (6 feet) tall. While it might indeed be helpful, and life might be in your favor if you are, there are always outliers, given that the smallest player in the NBA, Muggsy Bogues, was 1.6 meters (5.25 feet). If you feel a desire to slip into your sports shoes and compete with the best athletes in the world now, I am not going to hold you back. But I will bring some realism into the equation. We all operate within our genetic and socio-economic boundaries. Becoming one of the best athletes might not be your best course of action. However, there might be a path ahead for you to turn your life into an outstanding experience.

For some people, it is easier to adopt certain ideas if they are coated in scientific, mystical, or magical names, such as „quantum field", „genetic memory", or „energy vibration". Not only do these terms hold different meanings in physics, but they are also used to create an impression of being more scientific or mystical in the reader's mind. This does not make the effects more real, but it eases the burden of explanation from the writer, as well as makes it easier for the reader to believe them. This will work for many people just fine, but it always triggered my bullshit receptors.

Don't worry; there's no quantum wizardry here. I'm not going to tell you to align your chakras with Saturn's Wi-Fi signal. This is more about practical tools than cosmic mysteries. However, you will find that there is an element of mysticism in these pages. But as I am only a layman myself, you will have to excuse my shortcomings.

1 Nurture
Growing up in chaos

The earliest years of my life were energetic and full of the simple joys that came with growing up on a farm. By all outward appearances, it should have been a good life: we had open fields to explore, food always on the table, the promise of a decent education, and the freedom to play outside all day. I was part of a large family with five children, a setting that might evoke images of warmth and unity. Yet, beneath this seemingly idyllic surface, deeper tensions simmered, shaped by the fervent religious atmosphere of our home.

Perhaps you've experienced something similar. A life that looked fine from the outside, where basic needs were met, yet something felt fundamentally wrong underneath. The disconnect between appearance and reality can be one of the most confusing aspects of growing up in dysfunction.

Religion was lived and breathed in our home. One might naturally assume that devout faith inspires moral character, compassion, and better human beings. However, there is likely no more effective antidote to that belief than witnessing how religious devotion coexists with deep familial dysfunction. In fact, the religious environment may have compounded our problems rather than alleviating them. There was a masking mechanism at play, one that allowed harmful patterns to hide behind a façade of piety.

This dynamic is especially evident when one or more family members embody traits reminiscent of the Old Testament God, a figure whose behavior has been described by Richard Dawkins with scathing clarity. He wrote: „The God of the Old Testament is arguably the most unpleasant character in all fiction: jealous and proud of it; a petty, unjust, unforgiving control-freak; a vindictive, bloodthirsty ethnic cleanser; a misogynistic, homophobic, racist, infanticidal, genocidal, filicidal, pestilential, megalomaniacal, sadomasochistic, capriciously malevolent bully." Take a moment to consider these words. They don't just describe a fearsome deity from ancient texts; they also paint a stark portrait of a narcissistic personality. Fortunately, my family did not enact genocide. At least not yet.

I want to stress that there is nothing inherently wrong with having faith in a higher power or believing whatever resonates with you. This book isn't a takedown of religion. Instead, it's a personal narrative referencing what I experienced. Your beliefs, whatever they may be, might even make this story more intriguing for you. I am not claiming that religion itself is at fault; I'm pointing out how, in my particular household, spiritual doctrine intertwined with dysfunctional behavior to create confusion and pain.

1.1 Navigating Chaos and Building Resilience.

Growing up in a large family where religion seemed to justify emotional turbulence created a strange environment. On the one hand, there were moments of normal childhood play and even glimpses of gentler role models. My father and older brother, for instance, showed me another way of being. These contrasts were vital, as without them, I might never have realized that the relentless chaos, threats, and screaming were not how things had to be.

If you grew up in a similar environment, you might recognize this pattern. Perhaps you also had someone who showed you that life didn't have to be constant turmoil. Or maybe you're still searching for that contrasting perspective. These gentle role models, however small their influence, can plant seeds of awareness that bloom years later.

As children, we often sense something is fundamentally wrong, though we lack the words to name it. We assume our circumstances are simply how the world works. This dawning awareness sharpens over time, often shaped by the volatile dynamics within our households and the rigid expectations of those around us.

Within our family, the household descended into a frenzy whenever someone failed to behave according to certain members' expectations. Among those who shaped this reality was my mother, whose way of relating to the world followed a strict internal logic. In her framework, relationships functioned as transactions rather than personal connections. She did not perceive this as harmful; to her, it was simply the way things were. She operated according to control, obligation, and hierarchy rather than mutual care.

If I met her expectations, I was tolerated, perhaps even momentarily praised. If I failed, I was discarded emotionally or subjected to outbursts meant to realign me with her needs. But in her perception, this was not malice. It was simply how things were supposed to be. Any suffering she caused was either denied, reinterpreted, or reframed as my fault. Narcissists confabulate, constructing narratives where they are always justified, even when their actions inflict undeniable harm. It was only later that I realized her version of reality was not just different from mine, but fundamentally incompatible with genuine human connection.

Threats would rain down, and the shouting would erupt with such force that it could make the banshee of Irish folklore seem like a mere schoolgirl. It was a life lived on emotional eggshells. To cope, negative behaviors emerged as survival mechanisms. When trapped, we adapt, even if those adaptations ultimately harm us.

This is something only those who have endured narcissistic abuse can truly grasp. It distorts your sense of self and forces you into a reality that only exists in their minds. To outsiders, it's invisible, almost unimaginable. But for those who have lived it, the weight of that manipulation is all too real. Yet something resisted. Whether it was sheer luck, quiet defiance, or the influence of those who showed us another way, that resistance, however small, could be enough to break free eventually. We all carry this capacity for resistance, even when we don't recognize it at first. Amid this resistance, certain moments of solitude offer glimpses of clarity that guide the path forward.

Moments of quiet clarity appear in unexpected places. One memory stands out. A red sand hill near our home became a sort of private testing ground for my thoughts and courage. I would climb to the top, inhale the dusty air, and race back down, letting my limbs sink into the soft sand, briefly free from all the noise. The thrill of challenging my physical limits flushed my brain with excitement and adrenaline, temporarily freeing me from the web of social complexity I found at school and home.

It was on that hill, while pausing to catch my breath and prepare for another descent, that I wrestled with questions about social hierarchies. At school, I was not popular, at least that was my perception. Some family members, following their distorted logic, had offered advice on manipulating social structures to „bend" people's will. Yet this advice never felt right to me; it seemed unnatural and profoundly exhausting.

Standing there, overlooking the farm and feeling the grit of the sand under my fingertips, I asked myself why I should contort my behavior just to please others. What if, instead of trying to conform to these skewed patterns of power and status, I simply abandoned the concept altogether? I decided then that all people are equal beneath the sun and that chasing after popularity by dishonest means was a futile endeavor. With that realization, it was as if a massive weight had been lifted off my shoulders. I could return to my climbing and leaping, unburdened by the need to impress or dominate. In the years to come, this mindset would help me form authentic friendships. These were connections based on mutual respect and understanding rather than fear or manipulation. This shift in perspective, born on that sandy hill, revealed the transformative power of letting go.

This turning point taught me the power of letting go. Too often, we change only when the burden of carrying something becomes overwhelming. Had I continued striving for social standing through deceit, I would have broken under the weight of my own inauthenticity. Instead, I chose truth and simplicity. It marked one of my first real steps toward self-determination, a quiet rebellion against the dysfunctional patterns I had witnessed in my home.

Such realizations, small as they may seem, accumulate over time. They form the backbone of resilience. Without them, we remain trapped, just another piece of the family puzzle, blindly continuing the cycle. Instead, moments like the red sand hill, along with the decisions we make there, offer us crucial footholds in our journey toward greater emotional freedom.

1.2 Early Coping Mechanisms

Too often, meaningful change only occurs once the burden of carrying old patterns becomes unbearably heavy. The more stubborn we are, the longer we wait until, eventually, something breaks in a way we can't easily mend. In my upbringing, there was a perpetual atmosphere of guilt. It felt as if I could never measure up to what my family or God demanded. As a child caught in an abusive dynamic, feeling victimized was almost unavoidable. It's a natural reaction, yet carrying this victim mentality into teenage and adult years becomes a self-made prison. We relinquish all power to the abuser—past or present—by maintaining that victim narrative. If we're not responsible for our circumstances, we also cannot change them.

By my teens, I had absorbed many of the negative patterns displayed by family and friends. This is what children do; they observe the adults around them and model their behavior. But once we reach adulthood, clinging to childhood excuses no longer serves us. Consider encountering someone who, despite being fully grown, behaves like a spoiled child. Would you take their traumatic childhood into account, or would you simply keep your distance, recognizing that this person brings chaos and unreasonable demands into your life? Trauma does not grant perpetual leniency. In fact, emotionally intelligent people tend to distance themselves from those who refuse to grow, as true emotional intelligence includes knowing when to avoid self-inflicted disaster. By remaining stuck in old victimhood narratives, we repel positive influences, like good friends, reliable business partners, and loving romantic interests.

Unfortunately, some never break free from these patterns and instead entrench themselves deeper in them. My sister's endless lawsuits against my brother, built on fabricated grievances, showed how narcissists cling to victimhood to control others. Narcissists and those deeply steeped in dysfunctional thinking often rewrite events in their minds, justifying even the most irrational actions as necessary or righteous. Watching this unfold reinforced what I already suspected: some people will go to extreme lengths to maintain their version of reality, even if it means dragging others through unnecessary chaos. Such destructive patterns, rooted in dysfunctional thinking, often manifest as persistent behavioral challenges.

Compounding this problem, certain behavioral patterns acted like those little pop-up ads: annoying, persistent, and always in the way of what you're trying to accomplish. One that plagued me as a teenager and college student was attention-related issues, often summed up as ADHD. This wasn't just a matter of scattered focus but a byproduct of the chaos I had endured. At home, whenever the „screaming banshees" resumed their relentless noise, there was nowhere to hide. Even something as simple as locking my bedroom door was not possible, as the keys had been removed. Why? Because privacy provides a tool to escape the constant barrage of emotional violence. And nothing terrifies a narcissist more than abandonment or the idea that someone might choose solitude over their tyranny.

Narcissists, shaped in their own childhood by fear and insecurity, desperately attempt to keep others close through control. Instead of fostering love or creating pleasant experiences to ensure companions stay willingly, they limit avenues of escape. They do this materially (removing keys, sometimes removing financial independence) and emotionally (threatening, guilting, manipulating). Trapped as a child in such an environment, direct confrontation—fight—often ended poorly due to power imbalances. Flight—escaping, was systematically denied. With no healthy option to deal with stress, the only remaining choice was a third coping mechanism: tuning out.

Dr. Gabor Maté captures this dynamic precisely: „If I were to stress you right now, create stress, emotional difficulty or tension for you, what would be your options? ... You could fight back, flight or fight. But what if you didn't have those options? Then you're stuck. And now, what does the brain do when you're stuck like that? It tunes out ... In other words, it's a coping mechanism."

This forced „tuning out" often manifested as inattention, difficulty focusing, and other ADHD-like symptoms. To escape reality further, video games became a refuge. Their rapid pace and endless stimulation drowned out the negative thoughts looming beneath the surface. Social media provides a similar escape for many. This offered temporary peace, but it was also training the brain to constantly seek distraction. Brains learn what we repeatedly do. Train yourself to focus deeply, and you become better at focusing. Train yourself to numb out with screens, and you grow more adept at avoiding problems. Over time, habits of avoidance become entrenched. While it's understandable for a child facing unbearable stress, continuing this pattern into adulthood sabotages growth. It's easy to blame ADHD for not achieving goals, but using it as a perpetual excuse ensures stagnation. These patterns of avoidance, while understandable in childhood, left lasting scars that shaped the search for a better way forward.

Scars from such childhood turmoil appear in countless forms. As Leo Tolstoy wrote: „All happy families are alike; each unhappy family is unhappy in its own way." My family's unhappiness became both a curse and, strangely, also a blessing. Something was deeply wrong, though the root cause wasn't clear yet. This uncertainty propelled a quest for a better way of navigating through life.

Watching others glide through life as if they were in a ballroom dance, while I was over here doing the cha-cha with a broomstick and tripping over my own feet. While I thrashed and struggled, they laughed easily, achieved smoothly, and appeared deeply connected to themselves and others. It seemed so unfair. How did they move so lightly while shame, fear, and frustration weighed everything down? Looking back, their ease wasn't a natural gift; it was something forged by understanding, honesty, and a willingness to face discomfort. Often, it is pain—the rock bottom—that forces us to question everything. Pain can become a catalyst, a strange teacher that propels growth.

This book emerged from that realization, aiming to use suffering as a stepping stone toward a more effortless life. Taking full responsibility for circumstances freed me from being a passive victim. It was painful because there was no longer an option to blame others entirely. But it also gave a sense of power. Without ownership over our lives, we remain puppets in someone else's play, always at the mercy of their whims. Accepting responsibility is hard because it strips away excuses. However, it also places the steering wheel back in your hands, allowing you to choose your path forward.

1.3 Growing Out of It

Most of us do not choose change unless we feel we must. If life is just comfortable enough, we remain as we are. Yet, the moment we commit to improving our circumstances, we discover that stepping out of our comfort zone is necessary. Every content, resilient individual you meet has faced challenges, and this outcome is not the result of a lucky draw. As Seneca wrote, *„No man is more unhappy than he who never faces adversity. For he is not permitted to prove himself."* This shift in perspective reframes hardship as a crucible where personal growth, courage, and adaptability are forged. Throughout these pages, I will show not only how to confront challenges more effectively but also how to cultivate a lasting peace of mind that heightens the depth and quality of our lives. This journey of growth begins in childhood, where our earliest experiences shape the challenges we must later overcome.

In the first half of life, we are inevitably dependent on others, such as parents, guardians, or caretakers, who assume responsibility for our welfare. In exchange, we sacrifice freedom for protection and guidance. Ideally, this arrangement is temporary and meant to prepare us to stand on our own. Unfortunately, many parents project their unprocessed desires and traumas onto their children, burdening them with demands they should never have to carry. Over time, we must learn to shield ourselves from these distorted expectations and find our own way.

Carl Jung captured this life journey succinctly: „*The first half of life is devoted to forming a healthy ego, the second half is going inward and letting go of it.*" Early on, we're shaped by our environment, for better or worse. Later, to evolve, we must peel back those layers, releasing what no longer serves us. If parents or society push too hard in one direction by imposing their wounds, insecurities, or unrealistic standards, we face a complex dilemma.

Some people become chronic people-pleasers, ever seeking approval they never received as children. Others mimic the controlling behavior of their parents, lashing out at themselves or others. Still, others remain stuck in a state of conflict, unsure how to set boundaries or protect their inner peace. At the far extreme, there are those whose parents never gave them real challenges to overcome, leaving them with low self-esteem and no evidence of their own resilience. Parenting is fraught with pitfalls, and while some parents manage better than others, none are perfect.

In my own case, I'm grateful for the trials I endured. Although they had the potential to break me, facing adversity helped me grow. Suffering, when processed properly, leads to wisdom. True wisdom arises when once-painful memories lose their emotional grip. Without that release, suffering repeats in endless cycles. By transmuting traumatic experiences into learning experiences, we gain a valuable form of resilience. When confronted with a similar struggle later, instead of reacting from a wounded place, we respond intelligently, applying knowledge rather than pain. In this way, suffering can become the furnace that forges strength and insight.

Many of our daily actions arise from unconscious habits formed through past experiences, especially when shaped by trauma or persistent stress. Recognizing these habitual patterns is crucial but changing them effectively often requires practical tools that help you transform small, everyday behaviors. While this book guides you deeper into inner mastery and awareness, books like James Clear's Atomic Habits are a valuable companion resource if you seek practical strategies to reshape these daily routines and create lasting change intentionally.

Consider the myriad negative thoughts: fear, anger, guilt, anxiety, depression, frustration, jealousy, grief, loss, perfectionism, disappointment, feeling overwhelmed, feeling of lack, blame, drama, control, self-importance, conceit, and judgment. These can thrive only as long as we hold onto them. Let them go, and they dissipate, clearing space for healthier emotions. Negative emotions often interlink: feeling a sense of lack might ignite jealousy or envy, which leads to frustration, anger, and eventually blame and attempts at control. Without realizing it, we escalate from subtle discomfort to full-blown chaos simply by not releasing the initial negativity.

19

Observing our emotions early teaches us to trace them back to their source. Often, anger or disappointment stems from unfulfilled expectations we set for others or ourselves. If these expectations go unmet, we respond emotionally. Yet, as Anthony De Mello puts it: „*I want to tell you exactly how you're expected to behave, and you'd better behave as I have decided, or I shall punish myself by having negative feelings.*" It's a humorous yet painfully accurate assessment. We use unmet expectations as an excuse to inflict suffering on ourselves, holding onto hot coals of anger or resentment as if to prove a point. They may have lit the fire, but is it their fault or yours if you are burning your fingers and refusing to let go?

One might think the solution is to have no expectations at all. While appealing in theory, it's not realistic. Expectations are part of how we navigate reality. If someone regularly fails to keep promises, our expectation adjusts accordingly, and we expect less from them. Managing expectations fluidly, without harsh judgment, allows us to remain flexible. Instead of clinging to old expectations and getting burned, we drop them like hot coal and adapt. This requires acknowledging that our judgment, not the other person's behavior, caused the pain. The ego detests admitting it could be wrong. Yet, learning to accept our fallibility and forgive ourselves or others is a potent antidote to emotional suffering.

Underlying all these transformations is a commitment to truth. Improving our human condition means facing reality, no matter how uncomfortable it may be. When the truth hurts, many will lie to themselves and to others to escape that immediate pain. This tactic only leads to more suffering in the long run. Establishing a habit of honesty, even when it involves loss or discomfort, shields us from greater turmoil down the line. Tragically, many people consider small lies harmless or beneficial in the short term, unaware that every lie strengthens a habit of untruthfulness that can ultimately distort their understanding of themselves and the world. Most of the lies we tell are to ourselves, and this self-deception is a formidable barrier to growth. By embracing honesty as a guiding principle, we align our actions and emotions with reality. In doing so, we dismantle the internal illusions that keep us trapped. Overcoming this barrier requires a commitment to truth, a principle that guided my path out of childhood chaos.

My childhood, steeped in religious fervor and familial dysfunction, was far from the paradise it might have appeared at a glance. Yet, it set me on a path toward self-awareness and authenticity. The lessons learned from those early struggles serve as a compass for personal liberation. These lessons include dropping destructive expectations, facing adversity, taking responsibility, embracing truth, and forgiving myself and others. By sharing this journey, I hope to illuminate a route that anyone, regardless of their past, can follow toward freedom and inner peace.

2 Trauma
Understanding Its Grip on the Self

Trauma is an inescapable part of the human experience. It shapes us in ways we often don't realize, influencing our perceptions, decisions, and relationships. But here's a truth we seldom discuss: trauma is not merely something to survive. It can also be a doorway, a challenge that, when faced, leads to profound growth and transformation. The question isn't whether trauma is valid; it is. The question is what we choose to do with it. Will we let it weigh us down, or will we transform it into a source of strength and wisdom?

Imagine yourself standing in the aftermath of a storm, surveying the wreckage. At first, it seems overwhelming.

But look closer. Amid the debris lies the foundation for something new, something stronger. Trauma works in much the same way. It shakes us, tests us, and leaves scars. Yet those scars can become stories of resilience if we're willing to do the work. This work of rebuilding begins with understanding how trauma lingers not just in our minds but in our very bodies.

Physically, trauma roots itself in our bodies as much as in our minds. Have you ever noticed your heart racing when you hear a particular song or your breath catching at a familiar scent? That's your body remembering. When a situation reminds us of a past trauma, our survival instincts kick in: heart pounding, muscles tensing, breath quickening. This fight-or-flight mode was crucial when our ancestors faced life-threatening dangers, but in our modern world, it can hijack our daily lives and relationships.

Trauma has a sneaky way of weaving itself into our lives, often without us even realizing it. It can show up as relentless anxiety, a harsh inner critic, emotional outbursts, or strained connections with those we love. We tell ourselves stories to justify these patterns, blaming circumstances or thinking, „This is just who I am." But here's the empowering truth: trauma doesn't get the final say. It's not your destiny—it's your challenge. And when you choose to face it, you unlock the potential for growth, resilience, and a life filled with deeper meaning and connection. Yet, in our pursuit of growth, we must also recognize when healing becomes a trap of its own.

However, as important as the healing journey is, there comes a point when we must realize we're already enough, imperfections and all. Ironically, the never-ending pursuit of healing can become a subtle way of reinforcing our sense of being broken. I once stumbled across a playful social media post that simply said, „Stay Damaged." It was both funny and surprisingly profound, reminding me how absurd it can be to endlessly chase perfection. Maybe the greatest healing comes not from fixing every wound but from embracing ourselves fully, scars included.

2.1 From Survival to Transformation

Think of those who've faced unimaginable pain and emerged stronger, wiser, and more compassionate. These are the people who refuse to let their past define them. They've shifted their perspective, viewing their experiences not as a curse but as an opportunity for transformation. This shift, moving from victim to survivor and from broken to rebuilding, is the essence of post-traumatic growth. This transformative journey, known as post-traumatic growth, hinges on a fundamental change in how we view our pain.

Post-traumatic growth (PTG) represents the remarkable capacity of humans to find meaning and resilience in the face of adversity. It begins when we reframe our perspective, replacing the question, „Why did this happen to me?" with, „How can I grow from this?" Of course, this is easier said than done. Healing from trauma isn't a straight line. It's a chaotic journey full of setbacks and breakthroughs, and sometimes, we need help navigating it.

During an ayahuasca ceremony, I vividly experienced this truth. As the powerful plant medicine took effect, dark, intimidating figures appeared before me, embodying my deepest fears. Initially, terror surged through me, but rather than resisting or indulging in panic, I decided to sit quietly, observing and accepting these figures as manifestations of past trauma and internalized fear. In that moment of surrender and acceptance, these once-terrifying presences transformed into something neutral, even friendly. The fear dissolved instantly, replaced by a profound sense of peace. This taught me that when we sit patiently with our fears and observe them without judgment, acknowledging they stem from past rather than current threats, they lose their power and vanish. This lesson in facing fears resonated deeply, much like the radiant energy of a friend I met years later in college.

I met a remarkable human while in college: Isabelle. She was a shining light, the kind of person who could walk into a room and make everyone feel like life just got a little brighter. She always had a smile on her face, and her energy would radiate into the room. Isabelle and I shared countless adventures. We were like Bonnie and Clyde, except our escapades didn't involve bank robberies but rather underground raves in forgotten forests and dimly lit warehouses. Surrounded by fairies, druids, and wandering souls, we became part of this surreal, ethereal world. On the dance floor, we'd clown around or try to outdo each other with absurdly elaborate dance moves. It didn't matter who was watching because, in modern terms, „she was a vibe." Yet, life has a way of testing even the brightest spirits, as I saw when Isabelle faced an unexpected challenge.

Now, imagine the cognitive dissonance my friend Victoria experienced when she met Isabelle in her dancing class, only to find a withdrawn wallflower instead of the radiant soul I described. In her mid-twenties, Isabelle was struck with a sledgehammer in the form of a cancer diagnosis. What a cruel twist of fate. Just as she was carving out her independence, she suddenly found herself dependent on friends and family again. Her once-sparkling personality dulled, replaced by exhaustion and a blank expression. Even playing a simple card game could leave her utterly drained. Treatments battered her body, and her confidence crumbled. She withdrew from her friends, her laughter gone, her energy depleted. She felt like she had lost herself, reduced to a shadow of the person she once was.

The road ahead wasn't just difficult. It was brutal. Isabelle faced two stark choices: she could let bitterness consume her, sinking into the abyss of „Why me?" or she could take responsibility for her own well-being. She could remain stuck, lamenting the unfairness of it all, or she could forgive both the people who failed to understand her pain and the world that seemed so indifferent to her suffering. She had to let go of her expectations of how life should be and focus on reclaiming her vitality, one painstaking step at a time.

Her journey was nothing short of a baptism by fire. It burned away her illusions and stripped her down to the raw essentials of who she was. She had to relearn patience, resilience, and the courage to face life's endless uncertainties. Watching Isabelle navigate this path reminded me of the story of Job from the Bible, a man whose faith was tested in the harshest of ways. God allowed everything to be taken from Job, including his wealth, family, and health, as part of a questionable divine bet. Yet, even in his darkest moments, Job remained faithful. In the end, his faith was rewarded, and everything he lost was returned to him twofold. Isa's story felt like a modern echo of that tale, though her journey wasn't dictated by divine intervention but by her own resolve. Like Job, Isabelle's strength lay in her ability to release old burdens and embrace a new way of being.

Through years of grueling effort, Isabelle began to shed the expectations that weighed her down, like finally tossing out those jeans that hadn't fit since high school. As she let go, something shifted. The emotions that had been bottled up began to flow freely. Her smile returned, radiating with the same energy but carrying more depth, like a beautiful song played in a richer key. These days, her joy has evolved. Gone are the wild warehouse raves and tequila-fueled escapades. Now, it's all about yoga sessions and kombucha. A vibe shift, but with significantly fewer hangovers and far less glitter stuck in random places.

Much like Job and Isabelle, if we navigate trauma without letting it define us, we can emerge stronger, more resilient, and infinitely wiser. Patience doesn't come from a life of endless ease, and resilience isn't born in comfort. It's the challenges we face, the struggles we endure, and the pain we transform that shape who we become. The only promise I can give you is this: if you commit to becoming the best version of yourself, you'll live a life that's nothing short of astonishing. But if you choose to stay trapped in the shadows of your trauma, the alternative is as bleak as a festival with no music. At the heart of such resilience lies an understanding of trauma's deep imprint on our memories and bodies.

Trauma is an emotionally charged memory. These memories are powerful because they're not just stored in our minds but imprinted deeply in our bodies. They're formed when an experience elicits a significant emotional reaction, essentially locking the event into our subconscious. The stronger the emotion, the more intense the memory will be. Over time, these emotionally charged memories can influence our behaviors and perceptions without us even realizing it.

Not all trauma comes from events we consciously remember. Some of the deepest wounds are formed in the earliest years of life, before we even develop language to process them. These early experiences, such as an absent caregiver, prolonged stress, or medical trauma, don't leave behind clear memories, but they shape the nervous system in profound ways. The body remembers what the mind cannot, encoding fear, instability, or abandonment deep into our subconscious. This can manifest later in life as unexplained anxiety, difficulty forming healthy relationships, or an overactive stress response. Without realizing it, we may react to present situations based on wounds from a past we don't even recall. Healing these early imprints isn't about uncovering lost memories but about recognizing the patterns they create, soothing the nervous system, and learning to reparent the parts of ourselves that never felt truly safe.

However, the worst outcome is identifying with your trauma, allowing it to become a part of your identity. I speak from experience when I say that this mindset is destructive. The constant rumination, unresolved anger, frustration, guilt, or fear can all consume you. If you believe these feelings will never leave, then that belief may become your reality. This pain can spill over into your relationships, causing harm to others and eventually leaving you isolated. I've witnessed this firsthand in my own family and know how devastating it can be. Whether or not you believe you can let go of your emotionally charged memories, that belief will shape your future. To break free from this destructive cycle, we must approach healing with care and intentionality.

Overcoming trauma requires patience and a gentle approach. Imagine a horse terrified of carrots. Poor little fellow didn't get the best hand from destiny. You wouldn't just throw a salad at it; you'd ease it in with baby steps. Or, in this case, baby carrots. Instead, you'd create a safe environment and reintroduce the carrots gradually, soothing its nervous system along the way. Similarly, humans need a secure space and incremental steps to release the emotional charge of trauma and reframe their experiences. Trauma is an emotionally charged memory; once you release the emotional charge, it transforms into wisdom. Emotions cannot be controlled, but they can be guided. By understanding the motivations and mechanisms of our subconscious mind, we can learn why certain emotions remain stuck rather than flowing through us.

But here's the rub: letting go isn't always a clean break. Some emotions, like grief, shame, that gnawing anger you can't name, stick like burrs, resurfacing when you least expect it. You might sit there, watching them roll in, willing the weight to lift, but sometimes it just sits heavier.

That's not failure; it's the body holding onto what the mind wants to release. For me, it wasn't about fighting the storm. I let it rumble through, no judgment, just feeling it settle into the sand beneath me. Only then could I see it for what it was: an old echo, not my present. Detachment works, but sometimes you've got to lean into the mess first to loosen its grip. This process of detachment, while powerful, often requires practical steps to address emotions that linger stubbornly.

So how do you do it when the burrs won't budge? Start small: find where it lives in you. Is it a knot in your gut, a tightness in your throat? Breathe into it, not to fix it, but to sit with it, like you'd sit with a friend who's hurting. Some folks I've known scribble it out. Pages of jagged words, half-coherent rants about whatever's clawing at them until the pen slows and the ache dulls. Others just stay still, like I did, letting it wash through without a fight, no need to name it or shove it away. The raver dancing off their fear didn't just tweak their brain juice. They felt the beat, the sweat, the release. You don't need a warehouse or a pill, just a corner of quiet and the guts to face what's there, however you meet it.

This isn't pretty work, and it's sure as hell not linear. One day you're free, the next you're back in the muck. But each time you feel it through, it loses a bit of its hold. Think of it like peeling an onion, layer by layer, tears and all, until you hit something raw but real. That's where the wisdom hides, not in dodging the pain but in wrestling it into something you can carry lighter. For Isabelle, it was sobbing through chemo exhaustion until she could laugh again. For me, it was the sand under my nails and the quiet after the storm passed. It's yours to find, but you've got to dig your own way, no script required. These personal acts of facing trauma not only free us internally but also reshape how we move through the world.

This internal transformation inevitably changes the way we experience the outer world. It can feel as if the world punishes us for negative thought patterns and rewards us when we shift them. Several subtle mechanisms contribute to this phenomenon. A clear mind, free from negativity, allows intuition to assess situations more effectively. Your body language shifts, projecting a different energy that alters how others respond to you. Even the tone of your voice changes, leaving a more positive impression. Even your dog can sense when you've let go of negativity, and suddenly, you're getting tail wags instead of judgmental side-eye. The profound impact of aligning your inner world with positive growth isn't taught in schools, but it should be. Changing your internal dynamics not only improves your emotional experience but also sets you on a new path in life.

Wisdom arises when you have memories of intense experiences that no longer carry emotional weight. Seldom can knowledge transform into wisdom without suffering. But going through suffering and transforming it into wisdom is the forge that builds resilience. Letting go of the emotional charge is essential; otherwise, it will lead to repetitive suffering. Wisdom means that when we are faced with a similar experience, we do not react from a wounded place due to our traumas but instead respond based on knowledge. Making your traumatic experience into a learning experience is the key to wisdom.

Remember: „Stay Damaged"—a playful reminder from Namaste Bae not to take your healing journey so seriously that you forget you're already enough as you are.

3 The Body
The Foundation

Before we delve into what constitutes our human experience, it is essential to discuss our physical vehicle: the body. It's not just a sack of bones and muscles; it's the foundation for every thought, feeling, and action we experience. There is an abundance of information and numerous paths to molding this vehicle. If life is a movie, your body is the screen. Neglect the screen, and even the best films become blurry and unwatchable.

Despite its undeniable importance, many people treat the body and mind as separate entities. Yes, everyone knows the brain resides in the body, but societal norms often reinforce the illusion of a mind-body divide. Let's set the record straight: Without a healthy body, it's nearly impossible to cultivate a healthy mind. This isn't a dismissal of the experiences of those with physical disabilities. Every living human relies on their body to interpret and navigate life. The brain, after all, is just another organ within this intricate apparatus. And if that apparatus is in poor condition, it's like trying to use a smartphone with a shattered screen—everything becomes harder to manage. Yet, despite this undeniable connection, many turn to external substances to manage their mental state rather than nurturing the body itself.

Modern culture has introduced us to countless ways of altering our perceptions and moods. From caffeine to alcohol, nicotine to prescription medications, substances are often seen as quick fixes for mental or emotional challenges. These substances can change your brain chemistry temporarily, offering fleeting relief or bursts of energy. However, they come at a cost: dependence, withdrawal effects, and often a worse state of mind than where you started. Fortunately, there's a more sustainable way to shift your mental state, one that lies within your body's capabilities.

Here's the remarkable truth: your body holds the key to altering your brain chemistry naturally. By engaging in movement, adopting healthy postures, and maintaining physical vitality, you can not only change your emotional state but also enhance how others perceive you and, perhaps most importantly, how you perceive yourself.

This isn't about perfection or unattainable standards. It's about understanding that the body is both the foundation and the gateway to a better life. Good posture, regular exercise, and physical engagement aren't just things to check off a list but rather tools for emotional balance, mental clarity, and even self-empowerment.

We've mastered the art of excuse-making when it comes to exercise: „*Too tired,*" „*Too busy,*" or the classic „*My gym clothes are in the laundry.*" But research doesn't lie: regular physical activity can outperform Prozac in improving mental health. In fact, exercise is often the most effective and least utilized prescription for a happier, healthier life. Unfortunately, our healthcare system rarely prioritizes it. Despite this evidence, the medical system often overlooks exercise in favor of quicker, less transformative solutions.

Doctors are more likely to write a prescription for medication than to tell you to lace up your sneakers. Why? Because prescribing a pill is easier than having a difficult conversation about personal responsibility. In fact, it would be hardly imaginable for a doctor to tell you that you are responsible for your own life. Many patients would likely be upset about a doctor as insensible. As a doctor, it is just the easiest path to prescribe a pill instead of explaining how a patient needs to take responsibility for their body. Embracing this responsibility opens the door to profound changes, starting with how we carry and care for our bodies.

Taking care of your body doesn't just affect your physical health; it directly impacts your emotions and mood. Posture, for example, plays a surprisingly significant role. Standing tall with your shoulders back doesn't just make you look confident but also sends a signal to your brain that you've got things under control. Good posture enhances breathing, improves oxygen flow, and boosts energy levels. On the flip side, slouching restricts breathing, reduces oxygen intake, and fosters fatigue or even sadness. Research confirms that adopting a confident stance can release mood-enhancing neurotransmitters like serotonin and dopamine, while poor posture can spike stress hormones like cortisol.

Think about it: When you see someone dancing joyfully down the street, don't you assume they're happy? That's because it's nearly impossible for the mind to act against the body. When you move with energy and openness, whether through dance, a brisk walk, or playful movement, your mood inevitably shifts toward happiness. Yet, society often discourages such joyful movement, prioritizing a misguided sense of seriousness over vitality.

Our culture often equates seriousness with responsibility, but what if this relentless seriousness is the most irresponsible way to live? We don't become old, fragile, and miserable because it's inevitable; we become so because of our decisions. Sedentary lifestyles, which gained traction with the rise of agriculture and later with modern technology, have robbed us of vitality. We've convinced ourselves that physical activity is no longer necessary for survival. However, engaging with nature, like any other animal, is crucial.

Every mountain climber, runner, or surfer will tell you about the sheer joy of engaging with the world physically. Movement connects us to life. I doubt that anyone would argue that staying in motion while becoming older is a good thing. Some, however, might argue that at some point, we will just disintegrate regardless of all the effort. But why would it matter that we are all under the wheels of time? If you maintain your well-being throughout your life, it is worth all the effort. Why would you give up on existence before your timely end?

3.1 The Power of Movement and Nutrition

Imagine your body as a brilliant, untapped orchestra waiting for you to pick up the baton. Whether you're hitting the basketball court, gliding into a yoga flow, or grooving to music in your living room, movement is the magic that awakens your physical and mental harmony. It doesn't matter what you choose. What matters is that you move.

If you are not feeling physical discomfort once a day, you will lose the most important effect of working out, as this trains the resilience of body and mind. Your body is an incredible machine, capable of adapting and growing stronger with each challenge. Push yourself, whether through stretching after a long day or trying a new sport, and watch as your mind follows suit. Flexibility in the body breeds flexibility in thought and emotion.

Personally, I've found that no single sport can address all aspects of physical health. Surfing, for example, works wonders for my back muscles, but I complement it with other exercises to keep everything in balance. Even on days when all muscles feel exhausted, embracing the discomfort of stretching remains valuable. Why? Because the body thrives on engagement, and the mind benefits from the discipline of showing up.

Movement doesn't just keep you fit; it changes your brain chemistry. Those who dance with joy, walk briskly, or stand tall radiate an unmistakable vitality. It's nearly impossible to spot an old, depressed surfer, but spend time among sedentary retirees, and you'll notice the difference. Movement is more than exercise; it's your ability to express and respond to life. This vitality through movement is amplified when paired with the right nutrition, creating a powerful synergy for transformation.

Movement and nutrition are like two sides of the same coin, each amplifying the other's benefits. Whether you're flowing through yoga poses, sprinting on a track, or trying to master the art of dancing in your living room, movement energizes the body and sharpens the mind. But for movement to truly transform you, it needs the right fuel, and that's where nutrition steps in.

Think of your body as a high-performance car. Movement is the driving, the thrill of the open road, the joy of feeling alive. Nutrition is the premium fuel that keeps the engine running smoothly. You can't have one without the other, not if you want to reach your full potential. When you pair the two, you create a synergy that transforms not just your physical health but your mental and emotional well-being.

Sports and nutrition significantly impacted my personal development. In my family, there was never a strong emphasis on taking care of our bodies. Despite this, we were not extremely unhealthy either, because we were forced to work in the field after school and had food from local farmers. However, outside of work, we had little exercise, and our diet consisted largely of carbohydrates with no awareness of processed foods, still leading to an unhealthy lifestyle. Adding to this was the constant stress from family drama. Within the family and church, there was even a strong belief that the body should not matter. I vividly remember a sermon suggesting that focusing on your body was practically heresy because, apparently, lifting weights is a gateway to idolatry. What blasphemy this would be. In a sense, this perspective wasn't entirely wrong.

My initial motivation to learn about fitness and nutrition was driven by vanity. I wanted to look good and impress women. This one-dimensional approach to health overlooked many other important factors. But it was a start, and it led me towards a healthier lifestyle. The key takeaway here is that it doesn't matter what initially motivates you to explore fitness and nutrition; what matters is that you do. This exploration is the easiest way to transform your experience of life. Embracing a healthier lifestyle, regardless of the starting point, can lead to profound improvements in your overall well-being.

So here is a summary of the things I am looking out for in terms of nutrition:

- **Macronutrients**: Focus on fiber and protein. Fiber benefits gut health, influencing neurochemical production. 95% of serotonin is produced in the gut. Increasing fiber intake resolved some of my physical ailments. Protein is the most filling of the macros throughout the day. Just recently, it became abundant in wealthier societies. Not every source of protein is equally good; it's dependent on influences like hormones, heavy metals, and amino acid composition. Once fiber and protein needs are met, fats and carbohydrates usually follow suit. Not all fats are equal: Of 300 fatty acids, at least 24 are edible, half of those with adverse effects due to their structure. However, Omega-3 fatty acids, particularly α-Linolenic acid (ALA), are crucial for brain health. Consuming foods like avocado, hemp seeds, or olive oil daily is beneficial. It's advisable to reduce carbohydrate and fat intake due to their generally adverse effects.

- **Micronutrients**: Natural, not processed, fiber and protein-rich foods usually cover most micronutrient needs. While most supplements and superfoods are overrated, magnesium and vitamin D3 are worth noting. Magnesium aids in body regeneration, and vitamin D3, crucial for hormone production, is often deficient in non-tropical climates. Vitamin D3 is used in the synthesis of testosterone, as well as serotonin. Foods like blueberries and lion's mane mushrooms can boost Brain-derived neurotrophic factor (BDNF) and Nerve Growth Factors (NGF). However, finding what works for you is a personal journey. If you want to make sure that you have enough of these micronutrients, you could either do bloodwork or check the nutrients your meals have with tools that are available online.

- **Anti-nutrients**: Avoid foods with anti-nutrients, like French fries, which contain harmful compounds from high-temperature cooking of fats and carbohydrates. By frying, the nutrients are destroyed. The trans fats used have been shown to damage the brain, cause inflammation, and increase obesity. Even if good fat is used, the high temperature will oxidize it. The combination of fats and carbohydrates with temperatures above 120°C creates a component called acrylamide. Acrylamide has been shown to be carcinogenic, cause nerve damage, and cause metabolic disorders. In animal studies, it was found that this component may affect fertility and cause developmental defects. Many beloved foods, such as pizza, chips, and cakes, share these harmful components. Even though society promotes certain foods like breakfast cereals as healthy, science indicates otherwise.

Alcohol and cigarettes: Despite the known dangers of alcohol and cigarettes, cultural habits make it difficult to avoid them. It may come as a surprise to some, but habitual consumption of neurodegenerative substances is counterproductive. You are wasting your future for temporary pleasure.

While it could be interesting to explore how cacao, different algae, and mushrooms can have minor positive effects on health, this book does not focus on all the beneficial foods and supplements available. Many of these supplements are overhyped by marketing and won't be effective if you don't already have a healthy diet providing the right building blocks. Every human body is unique and has different needs, so finding what works best for you is a personal journey.

Changing eating habits is not an overnight change but several smaller steps. Reducing the consumption of most anti-nutrient foods takes time, and occasional indulgences will happen. After all, as part of the millennial generation, avocado on sourdough bread is our main source of food. If it weren't for this curse, we would, of course, be billionaires by now. Adopting these simple rules can improve your life, though they might not make your grandma stop offering you second helpings of pie.

Understandably, eating clean becomes hard, as the food industry purposefully creates addictive foods, which increase cravings. To describe this in the terms used by the food industry, they have taste institutes in which craving experts try to find the bliss point of food to create heavy users. If this sounds to you like an evil organization trying to create drug addicts, then you are not alone.

3.2 Recovery

If movement is the engine and nutrition is the fuel, recovery is the quiet mechanic that keeps everything running smoothly. Yet, for years, many treat recovery like an afterthought, an optional luxury for people with too much time on their hands. This is a mistake. Recovery isn't just important; it's essential.

In my early twenties, I invested significant effort into building a strong physique. I always attributed my slow progress to bad genetics. Despite working out consistently every day, I didn't gain much muscle. I tried to consume enough protein by eating curd and canned tuna since I couldn't afford high-quality food. I was convinced my diet of curd and canned tuna was a protein-packed strategy, but in hindsight, it was more of a culinary catastrophe lacking essential nutrients. Not only was my physique unimpressive, considering the work put in, but I also often experienced mental fog. Simultaneously, I had a habit of staying up late, playing video games, or partying. Looking back, it wasn't my workouts or even my makeshift diet that held me back. It was my neglect of recovery. I was addicted to short-term gratification, unwilling to admit that my lifestyle was sabotaging my long-term goals.

Recovery is when the magic happens. It's during rest, especially sleep, that your body repairs the tiny muscle tears caused by exercise, recalibrates your hormones, and consolidates new skills in your brain. Skip recovery, and your body becomes like a phone with too many apps running: slow, glitchy, and prone to crashing.

Sleep, in particular, is your body's nightly maintenance program. It's not just „shut-eye"; it's when you rebuild yourself. Those bursts of energy you feel at night? They're not an invitation to stay up late; they're signals for your body to regenerate. Without sleep, no amount of exercise or clean eating can compensate for the damage done by exhaustion.

Once the importance of recovery becomes clear, changes naturally follow. Setting a consistent bedtime, ideally before 11 pm, and switching devices to a red-light filter in the evenings can make a significant difference. It's not about achieving perfection but about finding a rhythm that supports your growth.

Recovery isn't just about sleep, though. Techniques like meditation, stretching, saunas, and even ice baths can help your body and mind reset. Some might scoff at the idea of elaborate bedtime routines, but even small adjustments, like unwinding with a book instead of a screen, can yield big results.

The neglect of recovery doesn't just impact your body; it can derail your mental and spiritual journey as well. During my early forays into meditation, I had one transformative experience that kept me chasing the same state of clarity. But I failed to replicate it consistently, partly because my mind was scattered by poor sleep habits. Recovery isn't just a break from effort; it's the fertile ground where effort takes root and flourishes.

Now, with a balanced recovery routine in place, everything has improved: my workouts, my focus, and even my emotional resilience. The lesson is clear: recovery is not the enemy of productivity; it's its greatest ally.

You don't need an oxygen chamber or a personal sleep coach to take recovery seriously (though wouldn't that be nice?). Start with small, manageable changes:

- **Sleep Hygiene**: Go to bed at a consistent time, reduce blue light exposure, and create a calming pre-sleep routine.
- **Active Recovery**: Incorporate gentle activities like yoga, stretching, or a leisurely walk on rest days.
- **Mental Recovery**: Give your brain a break through mindfulness practices or simple downtime.

By embracing recovery as a non-negotiable part of your routine, you'll not only unlock your body's potential but also enhance your overall quality of life. Growth, after all, doesn't just come from pushing harder; it comes from knowing when to step back and let your body do its work.

3.3 For the Science Enthusiasts

Resilience, for example, is influenced by the hormonal cocktail that our brain is soaking in. Low Cortisol, high Testosterone, Follicle-stimulating hormone (FSH), Luteinizing hormone (LH), Prolactin, sex hormone binding globulin (SHBG), Anti-Mullerian Hormone (AMH), Prostate Specific Antigen (PSA), to name a few of your hormones. Reading the list, you might have figured out that many of them are highly connected with your sexual hormones. It turns out that they make you resilient toward the storms of your life. Your immune regulation plays a big role as well by reducing inflammation within your body, which helps you deal with external stressors. This is based on High-Sensitive C-Reactive Protein (hsCRP), White Blood Cell Count (WBC), Neutrophils, Lymphocytes, Monocytes, Eosinophils, and Basophils. One of the key organs to building some of the most important markers is your liver, with markers like Gamma-glutamyl Transferase (GGT), Total Protein, Albumin, Total Bilirubin, Aspartate Transaminase (AST), Alanine Aminotransferase (ALT), and Alkaline Phosphatase (ALP). Then there is your autoimmune response, where we measure

Antinuclear Antibodies (ANA). We will probably find more markers in the future.

Testosterone, despite its negative image in society, is essential for both men and women, as estrogen is derived from it. High estrogen levels indicate to the body sufficient testosterone levels, which are crucial for muscle and bone health and resilience. It means that this hormone has a substantial impact on your path in life. However, environmental factors and diet can decrease these hormone levels, with some studies showing a 30% reduction in testosterone compared to our grandparents. Maintaining healthy testosterone and estrogen levels is essential for overall health and well-being. Key factors include:

1. Sleep: It is important to sleep before midnight and reduce sources of blue light before sleeping. This seems to be a big indicator of depression as well.
2. Food: Reduce phytoestrogen, Bisphenol A (BPA), sugar, alcohol, vegetable oils, and trans-fats in your food. Increase cholesterol, zinc, and DHEA-rich foods, as that is one of the most important building blocks for Testosterone. If you are not living in a sunny country, then you might also have insufficient amounts of vitamin D.
3. Working out big muscle groups will increase Testosterone.
4. Reduce toxins in your environment, like BPA, forever chemicals, and air pollution.
5. Reduce stress. We can reduce stressful situations but not fully remove them. However, we can change our response to the situations.

6. Do activities that increase testosterone and decrease stress, like ice baths, saunas, and massages.

7. Reduce radiation close to your groin or ovary, which also affects your Testosterone negatively.

There is confusion about cholesterol and heart health. While high LDL levels are linked to heart disease, cholesterol itself is vital for many bodily processes. LDL transports cholesterol to tissues, and problems arise when LDL levels are too high, blocking arteries. Studies show that dietary cholesterol, like that from eggs, doesn't significantly raise LDL levels. Instead, sugar intake seems to increase LDL levels. LDL is only produced when the tissues do not get enough cholesterol. There is some research claiming that the increase in LDL is based on mycotoxins. However, there seems to be no conclusive evidence of what the main cause of increased LDL is at this point. Understanding these complex interactions requires further research. However, this highlights that popular beliefs are not adjusted to the current science, and science can adapt with new information.

Our body influences our mind and well-being more profoundly than we often realize. When you crave cake, it's not actually „you" craving it. It's the bacteria in your gut. These microorganisms send signals to your brain, which then rationalizes this desire, convincing you that you want the cake. By choosing which bacteria to feed, through your diet and lifestyle, you can influence these cravings. This highlights that not all your thoughts are truly yours, as you are a host to billions of conscious organisms impacting your thoughts and well-being. Research shows that the gut microbiome, which can produce mood-affecting neurotransmitters like serotonin and dopamine, plays a crucial role in mental health. The gut-brain axis is a complex communication network linking your gut and brain, and it illustrates the bidirectional relationship between physical and mental health.

For science enthusiasts, the interplay of hormones, immune markers, and gut health is a treasure trove of discovery. But for the rest of us, the takeaway is simpler: you are creating your body every day. The food you eat, the way you move, and the environment you live in all contribute to this ongoing process.

When you bite into an apple, your body doesn't just absorb its nutrients. It transforms them into the building blocks of your well-being. This efficiency means that your job is simple: provide your body with what it needs and stay active. Fall in love with your body's incredible ability to regenerate and adapt, and you'll discover a profound change in how you feel and live.

3.4 The Nervous System

Healing is often seen as an intellectual or emotional process involving changing thoughts, shifting beliefs, or processing feelings. While these are important, true transformation is incomplete without addressing the nervous system. The body, after all, holds the imprint of every experience we have ever lived. If we want to free ourselves from suffering, we must learn to regulate the nervous system, allowing it to shift from survival into safety, from contraction into openness, and from reactivity into presence.

Many of the struggles we face, like chronic anxiety, emotional reactivity, difficulty trusting others, or a deep sense of unease, are not just psychological but physiological. The nervous system stores stress, trauma, and patterns of dysregulation. Even if we logically know that we are safe, the body may still be bracing for impact, caught in a loop of fight, flight, freeze, or fawn responses.

This is why intellectual insight alone is not enough. We cannot think our way into safety; we must feel it. Healing begins when we teach the body that it no longer needs to defend itself against threats that no longer exist.

The autonomic nervous system operates in two primary states: the sympathetic (activation, fight-or-flight) and the parasympathetic (rest, digest, restore). In a balanced system, we shift between these states as needed. However, unresolved stress and trauma can cause us to get stuck in hyper-vigilance or shut down, making it difficult to experience true presence and peace.

Regulating the nervous system means retraining it to access safety, allowing us to return to a baseline of calm rather than defaulting to stress and overwhelm. This process does not happen through force or willpower but through gentle, consistent practices that signal to the body: „You are safe. You can let go.“

Recent studies have shown that movement-based practices like yoga, running, and weightlifting are among the most effective ways to regulate the nervous system.

Yoga has been widely researched for its profound effects on nervous system balance. Research by Streeter et al. (2012) in *Frontiers in Human Neuroscience* found that regular yoga practice enhances vagal tone, increases heart rate variability (HRV), and improves autonomic nervous system balance, leading to greater emotional stability and stress resilience. Additionally, Pascoe et al. (2017) in *Psychoneuroendocrinology* reported that yoga significantly reduces cortisol levels, the stress hormone that perpetuates a chronic fight-or-flight state. Through breathwork, controlled movement, and mindfulness, yoga facilitates a shift into a parasympathetic state, where deep restoration occurs.

Running is another powerful tool for nervous system regulation. A study by Thayer & Lane (2009) in the *International Journal of Psychophysiology* found that aerobic exercise, particularly running, enhances heart rate variability (HRV), a crucial marker of parasympathetic nervous system activity. This suggests that running strengthens autonomic flexibility, helping the nervous system recover from stress more effectively. Furthermore, Hansen et al. (2004) in the *European Journal of Applied Physiology* demonstrated that endurance training improves vagal tone, enhancing emotional resilience and reducing the long-term effects of stress.

Weightlifting, often associated with strength and endurance, also plays a significant role in nervous system health. Heffernan et al. (2007) in *The Journal of Strength and*

Conditioning Research found that resistance training improves baroreflex sensitivity, an essential component of autonomic nervous system regulation, particularly beneficial for blood pressure control and cardiovascular stability. Additionally, Fisher et al. (2021) in *Frontiers in Physiology* examined the effects of strength training on cortisol regulation, showing that controlled resistance exercises help lower chronic stress hormone levels and promote a more balanced sympathetic-parasympathetic response. This suggests that lifting weights can counteract the body's stress response, leading to improved emotional regulation and resilience.

While movement is a critical component of nervous system balance, it is most effective when combined with other supportive practices:

- **Breathwork:** Techniques such as diaphragmatic breathing or extending the exhale help shift the nervous system into a parasympathetic state, signaling safety to the body.
- **Somatic Awareness:** Bringing attention to bodily sensations allows us to process stored tension instead of suppressing it. This can include shaking, stretching, or slow, mindful movement.
- **Cold Exposure & Heat Therapy:** Deliberate exposure to cold (such as cold showers) or warmth (like sauna therapy) helps train the nervous system to move between states with greater flexibility.
- **Grounding Practices:** Spending time in nature, walking barefoot, or simply feeling the weight of

the body against a surface helps bring awareness into the present moment.

- **Co-Regulation:** Safe, supportive relationships regulate the nervous system through connection. Being around calm and attuned individuals helps restore a sense of safety within ourselves.

- **Mindfulness & Meditation:** By cultivating stillness and awareness, we can observe our nervous system's fluctuations without getting caught in them, allowing us to respond rather than react.

One accessible yet powerful breathwork technique involves a simple rhythm: inhaling for two beats and exhaling for one beat. This practice, often referred to as „2:1 breathing," leverages the physiological connection between the breath and the vagus nerve, a key regulator of the parasympathetic nervous system. By emphasizing a shorter exhale relative to the inhale, this method gently stimulates the vagus nerve, promoting a calming effect that shifts the body out of a sympathetic, stress-driven state into a parasympathetic, restorative one. To practice, find a comfortable seated position, inhale deeply through the nose for a count of two, and exhale smoothly through the mouth for a count of one. Repeating this cycle for just a few minutes can lower heart rate, reduce muscle tension, and create a sense of grounded calm, making it an ideal tool for moments of anxiety or overwhelm.

Another distinct breathwork approach is the „double inhale" technique, which mimics the natural pattern of a sigh to quickly relax the nervous system. This method involves taking two short, consecutive inhales through the nose, almost like a quick sniff, followed by a deeper breath, before releasing a long, slow exhale through the mouth. The double inhale stretches the diaphragm and signals the brain to deactivate the stress response, while the extended exhale further reinforces a parasympathetic shift. This technique is particularly effective for immediate nervous system regulation, as it can be done in as little as one or two breaths, offering a rapid way to reset during high-stress moments or when feeling emotionally flooded.

Regulating the nervous system is not about avoiding stress or discomfort but about developing the capacity to navigate them with resilience. When we are regulated, we do not suppress emotions, but we also do not drown in them. We do not need constant external validation or distraction to feel okay. We become anchored within ourselves.

This is a fundamental step on the path of inner mastery. Without a regulated nervous system, self-awareness can feel overwhelming, and transformation remains elusive. But when the body learns to rest in safety, we can progress on the path of letting go of even those memories that are deeply buried in our subconscious.

The journey of self-mastery does not begin with controlling the mind. It begins with regulating the nervous system. Yoga, running, and weightlifting, as supported by multiple scientific studies, stand as some of the most effective ways to achieve this. Only then can we meet life with clarity, presence, and a deep, unshakable sense of peace.

3.5 The Legacy of Ignoring the Body

Let's talk about one of the great minds of the 20th century: Alan Watts. A philosopher, writer, and spiritual guide, Watts had a way of turning the complexities of life into profound simplicity. He was a giant in understanding the human mind, and his work has inspired countless spiritual journeys, including my own. Yet, for all his brilliance, even Watts couldn't escape the consequences of neglecting his body.

Watts died of heart failure, likely brought on by years of heavy drinking. No one can truly know what led him to drink or why he embraced habits that ultimately shortened his life. But one thing is clear: no amount of wisdom, knowledge, or eloquence can save you if the vessel carrying it is falling apart.

We've all experienced the seductive pull of short-term gratification. That dopamine hit from a glass of wine, a slice of cake, or a lazy afternoon in front of the TV. It feels good in the moment, but there's always a crash waiting on the other side. These fleeting pleasures can spiral into a cycle that leaves us physically and emotionally drained, a modern-day saṃsāra of indulgence and regret.

The takeaway here is painfully simple: your mind is only as good as the body that carries it. Watts's story isn't a cautionary tale meant to scare you into perfection; it's a reminder of the undeniable connection between our physical and mental states.

Imagine your body as a high-performance car. Would you pour sugar into the gas tank? Of course not. You'd fuel it with premium-grade gasoline, keep the engine well-oiled, and give it regular tune-ups. Treat your body with the same respect.

- **Move with Joy**: Find activities you genuinely enjoy—dancing, hiking, playing basketball—and make movement a part of your daily life.
- **Recover**: Prioritize sleep, relaxation, and recovery routines to give your body the maintenance it needs.
- **Fuel Wisely**: Focus on nutrient-rich foods, especially fiber and protein, and avoid the empty calories of anti-nutrients.
- **Avoid the Junkyard**: Skip habits that drain you in the long run, like excessive alcohol, sugar, and sedentary living.

Life doesn't give out awards for knowing everything about the universe while ignoring your body. You don't need to aim for perfection. Just focus on the process. Every small effort counts; over time, those efforts add up to a life that feels better, moves better, and thinks better.

Alan Watts's legacy reminds us of the mind's incredible power, but it also underscores the importance of honoring the body that houses it. Treat your body well, and it will repay you with the clarity, strength, and vitality you need to navigate this beautiful, messy, unpredictable life.

4 Your Experience
The Lens That Shapes Your World

Here is a bewildering human experience: Some of us seem to go by our own free will to places with deafening, loud, and screeching noises. Not only will the noise cause permanent damage to their hearing, but there are also explosions of light everywhere. The environment resembles a warzone more so than anything else in our usual experience. Not only is the environment scary, but it seems that of those who went, most are caught in a sort of hypnosis, forced to shake their body, looking like they have seizures. Others are petrified of what is happening but do not dare to express their discomfort, having an urgent desire to leave. Some feel that this environment allows them to express their desires for love. It seems like a demonic gathering of devils and witches, yet it happens every day in every bigger city around the globe. These events are usually pursued by humans being forced into adulthood, trying to show their last resistance towards a life of monotony forced upon them for their only god, mammon.

Yet it seems this absurd activity, which does seem so threatening, is one of the most exciting experiences many of us will have. Now, if you would ask one of these hypnotized dancers about their experience, they would say it was the most exhilarating and freeing experience they had. I personally can understand both perceptions of such events, having enjoyed my time on the dancefloor but also enjoying my peaceful and almost boring days, being committed to writing or coding. Both of these can give me an exhilarating experience I would not have believed achievable with mundane tasks.

My dancing counterpart of the past would be utterly bamboozled about the fever dream I am having right now, being secluded for days yet enjoying my time writing this. Be it partying, writing, coding, or just sitting silently in a room, it seems the same experience can be very differently perceived. Well, you might say it is dependent on the personality; this is a misconception that can limit you. Holding you prison to your own limiting beliefs. A realization that took me 37 years of my life to make.

4.1 The Pursuit of Life's Enriching Experiences

In essence, life is a collection of experiences. We pursue money, relationships, and health not for their own sake but because we believe they will enhance our journey. Yet, the key to a fulfilling life is not in chasing these tools but in consciously enriching the quality of our experiences. If we confuse these tools with our actual goal, we risk playing a game with different objectives. If we are chasing money or relationships, we will compromise our goals in life, changing the game we are playing. The rules of this new game will not be dictated by us but by someone else. Our primary focus should be on how to increase our life experience and move toward our purpose.

In our society, money is often highly valued, but in reality, it holds no inherent value. Money only has value because we assign it such. Imagine being stranded on an island with thousands of dollars in your bank account. You would gladly trade that money for drinking water and food. Here's another example: if a genie offered you more riches than the wealthiest person alive but only gave you three days to live, would you take it? Probably not. Yet, many people are willing to sacrifice their life experiences for the pursuit of money.

It's crucial to understand what makes an experience good or bad. Watching a sunset on the beach? Always a good experience, unless, of course, the mosquitoes decide you're the main course. However, our most memorable experiences often involve challenging endeavors. These could be climbing a mountain, running a marathon, building a company, or raising children. The key difference is that these experiences present challenges that we successfully overcome.

The loss of my father, someone I deeply loved, was one of the most painful experiences of my life. At the time, it felt like an unbearable weight, but in hindsight, it became a turning point. That loss forced me to confront my own fragility, reexamine my beliefs, and ultimately reorient my life's direction. As I grappled with grief, I realized that it was precisely these moments of profound pain that shaped the person I was becoming. The truth is, it's not our successes or easy moments that forge our character. It's our struggles, our heartbreaks, and our failures. These experiences test our resilience, reveal our vulnerabilities, and teach us lessons we can't learn any other way. Pain is not just an obstacle; it's often the forge where we are refined into stronger, wiser versions of ourselves. Without it, the story of who we are would be incomplete. A life without challenges would be very boring, after all.

4.2 States of Mind

Life often feels like a series of peaks and valleys, with moments of pure exhilaration juxtaposed against periods of struggle or monotony. Among these peaks, one state stands out as particularly transformative: the **flow state**. First described by Mihály Csíkszentmihályi, flow occurs when a challenge aligns perfectly with your skills, engaging you completely without overwhelming or boring you. In these moments, the boundary between you and the world fades, and time seems to stand still. It's the basketball player who can't miss a shot, the musician who is lost in their performance, or the writer whose words pour onto the page effortlessly. Flow feels magical, yet it is rooted in our psychology—a state where we feel happiness, confidence, and deep focus.

In that state, it seems like the borders between the world, and you seem to vanish. Any state outside of this flow state creates the dichotomy between you and me. After all, wouldn't existence be boring if it weren't for the duality between you and the world? Yet the same feeling of timelessness can enrich our existence substantially. These flow-states are the moments when we are not caught in our own thoughts, which allows us to have a break from our sometimes cumbersome existence. But exactly, these moments will inspire us to change something about our existence. And isn't this motivation nicer than being in so much pain that the only option is to change who you are?

Besides these intense moments we have in a flow state, we also need moments where we experience serenity, love, awe, inspiration, satisfaction, and contentment. These moments nourish our soul and let us recover. The goal is to maximize these positive experiences but also to have challenging experiences that engage us.

To achieve that, we will also need to minimize experiences that keep us in other states of mind. The most important ones among them are fear, guilt, anger, anxiety, depression, jealousy, grief, loss, perfectionism, victimhood, frustration, disappointment, judgment, feeling of lack, blaming, being dramatic, controlling, self-important, conceited, and feeling overwhelmed. These negative emotions drain our energy and space, preventing positive emotions from flourishing and hindering our growth.

You cannot control emotions, but you can influence whether you are triggered by them, and even if you are triggered, you can choose to respond thoughtfully to the emotion instead of reacting impulsively. By changing our internal framing, we can alter our responses to situations, resulting in different emotions and likely better outcomes. Emotions should not dominate our lives. They are transient, meant to be experienced and then let go. Holding onto any emotion, even positive ones, will result in pain.

When clinging to emotions, be it good or bad, we create expectations. While it is easy to see how negative emotions would be harmful, it is hard to see how good emotions would cause pain if you hold onto them. You will think of the good thing that once was or will come, but while it initially feels nice, it becomes too soon bittersweet. It pains you that, at this very moment, the thing is not like it is in your internal world.

The expectation of how the world ought to be and what the world really is will create friction within us. This is called cognitive dissonance. The Internal conflict occurring within us is the cause of pain. It means that your way of predicting the world is inaccurate. But because, in many cases, the things we initially learned in childhood or had sufficient evidence for were true and helped us to navigate through life, our ego will not let go easily of the ideas that don't benefit us. Most of our suffering is caused by cognitive dissonance. Here is the good news: nothing is permanent, even suffering. As one witty internet user once remarked, „*This too shall pass. It may pass like a kidney stone, but it will pass.*"

The only moment that will always be true is the present moment. And the more flexible we are in accepting circumstances, the faster we will adapt to environments that do not fit our expectations. Thereby reducing our suffering and leaving us with more capacity for other states of mind. Good emotions are fleeting by nature. If you try to hold on to them, they will vanish. We can't force them into existence. The only thing we can do is create space for them to arise. We only forgot that negative emotions are fleeting in nature as well. Our ego is holding onto the suffering and starts identifying with it. If it didn't have a meaning, what was the suffering for? Well, it had a meaning, it was meant to teach you not to hold onto it. If we get stuck on any moment in our life story, it will become suffering. It does not matter if it is good or bad.

„The desire for more positive experience is itself a negative experience. And, paradoxically, the acceptance of one's negative experience is itself a positive experience." Alan Watts described the irony of our desires beautifully. By letting go, negative emotions can transform into positive ones. If you pursue a feeling or a moment, you are telling your subconscious mind that you do not have the thing right now. The logical conclusion for your mind is that you cannot be happy right now, as you are lacking something. You are holding onto a moment that is not the current moment. The irony in this is that the future and the past are only constructs of your mind.

But why is it that there are some discomforting experiences, like working out or getting a tattoo, that do not seem to bother us while others do? In a sense, it is your decision on how you want to perceive the event. You consciously decided to get a tattoo or to work out. Often, this decision, however, is also ingrained into the mind by our repetitive behavior on how we deal with discomforting situations. We basically train ourselves to either deal well with discomfort or deal badly with it. Which is one of the reasons why you might engage with excitement in discomforting situations because you know it will aid you in the future when such or worse situations will unavoidably occur.

Once the memory is formed, it is based on the degree of pain the experience caused. The more painful the experience was, the more resistance will be. Emotions are meant to stay in motion, but by focusing on this emotion, either by re-experiencing it or forcefully suppressing it, prevents it from flowing through us. In the chapter on letting go, we will go into detail on how to deal with these states of mind.

Let's briefly address a word invented in 1936, „stress." Back then, it was defined as „the non-specific response of the body to any demand for change." While it might have its use for material sciences, it probably has adverse effects when used to describe the daily stress we are experiencing. Today, it is described as „a state of mental or emotional strain or tension resulting from adverse or demanding circumstances.". The emotional strain is caused by a discrepancy between reality as it is and reality as you expect, meaning you have cognitive dissonance. If this is a temporary state, then you are in pain. But if it is a lasting state, it means you are suffering.

It would have a very different ring in our ears if we call it suffering, and as such, it would warrant a very different response than what we are having now. It is utterly absurd that people proudly claim that they are stressed. Imagine if the world leaders, your boss, or friends would say that they are suffering instead of saying that they are stressed. It would have very different implications now, wouldn't it? If we become aware of our inner workings, however, we will reduce suffering and, therefore, stress naturally. No need for stress management or rubbing your ear while saying „*whoosah.*" (a reference from Bad Boys II)

4.3 Labels

From the moment we are born, the people around us such as parents, teachers, and peers begin shaping our sense of self. Labels are often assigned to us long before we understand their weight. These labels, whether positive or negative, become the lenses through which we view ourselves. Unless we become conscious of them, we may never question their validity, wrongfully assuming that this is who we are.

In school, for example, we were already getting used to being graded. The groups that surround us will claim that it is very important for our future. Creating a heavy load that we must carry. With many children, this will create resistance. Isn't it a reasonable reaction because who are you to define their worth? The assumption is that this would motivate them. But what if the child reacts with reasonable resistance to this concept? Instead of dealing with the resistance, we tell them they are just not smart enough. If the adults around you tell you that you are not smart enough, then that is what it must be, right? Our environment, especially the groups we identify with, will print a label on us, and we just accept it.

While in university, I worked as a math tutor and quickly noticed a pattern among the students who struggled. Most of them carried the belief that they were *„just not good at math"* or, even worse, *„not smart enough."* One parent even told her daughter, with good intentions, that their family was *„bad at math,"* as if it were a genetic curse. While this explanation may have soothed the child's initial frustration, it also reinforced a limiting belief: that she was inherently incapable. Teaching her mathematics became a battle not with the material but with her mindset. To help her, I first had to challenge that belief, encouraging her to see herself as capable. Once she embraced this new perspective, her resistance to learning gave way to genuine enthusiasm. By the end, she was outperforming her peers. Whether the belief endured, I can't say, but I hope the evidence she built for herself was enough to challenge that label in the future.

To change your experience in life, you must be willing to let go of the beliefs others have imposed upon you. This is no small task, because your ego will resist. Clinging to familiar narratives, no matter how limiting they are. But isn't it time to take back control? To redefine who you are, not by the labels others have given you, but by the person you aspire to be?

5 Ego
A Double-Edged Tool

Ego—what a fuzzy, elusive word. It's a term frequently tossed around, yet it often seems that everyone holds their own interpretation. In psychoanalysis, the ego is defined as the part of the mind that mediates between the conscious and the unconscious, playing a crucial role in reality testing, decision-making, and maintaining a sense of personal identity. But outside of clinical definitions, the ego can feel far less tangible. It operates in the background, influencing our perceptions, emotions, and behaviors, often without our explicit awareness.

To better understand this concept, consider the interplay between two aspects of your inner world: the creator of thoughts and the observer of those thoughts. Each person has a predominant mode of thinking. Some people think mainly in words, others in images, and still others through feelings. Of course, these modes can overlap, but there is usually one that stands out. In order to understand a person's mental framework, one might ask, *„Do you think in words, pictures, feelings, or some combination of these?"* If they answer *'memes,'* it's safe to assume you're talking to a millennial. Once the dominant mode is identified, a follow-up question can guide them into deeper self-inquiry:

- If you primarily think in words, ask yourself: „Am I the one speaking these words inside my mind, or am I the one listening to them?"

- If you think mainly in images, consider: „Do I identify with these pictures, or do I stand apart, simply observing them flash before my inner eye?"

- If you rely on feelings as your inner compass, reflect: „Am I my feelings, or am I the one perceiving these emotional currents within me?"

The truth is that you encompass both the role of creator and observer, regardless of whether your inner narrative unfolds through words, images, or feelings. You form these internal representations, and you also watch them happen. Yet, most of us tend to identify more with one aspect than the other. Some see themselves as the thinker or feeler, actively generating thoughts or emotions, while others may feel more like the observer. Neither identification is inherently right or wrong, but it's important to notice the implications. Understanding these internal dynamics can help us navigate our emotional landscapes with more awareness and less judgment. After all, judgment is just another emotional state, one that can hinder clear perception and lead to unnecessary suffering.

Observation without judgment allows us to recognize a pivotal truth: When we suffer, it is often because we are too enmeshed in our „*actor*" role, fully experiencing the emotional storms of life's dramas. Yet, there is another way to engage with reality. Imagine watching a tragic play on television. As a viewer, you find it moving or even entertaining, but you do not personally bear the pain of the characters. In your life, you play both the actor in the drama and the audience member in the stands. By shifting your perspective and choosing at times to be more like the observer, you can reduce the intensity of negative emotions and better understand the mental chatter that often accompanies stressful situations.

This shift is not about eliminating all thoughts or emotions; rather, it's about loosening the grip of the internal commentator. Notice how your internal monologue quiets down when you are fully immersed in enjoyable activities like dancing at a concert, singing with friends, or skiing down a snowy slope. The observer remains, but the voice that constantly judges and narrates recedes. It might seem that for optimal experience, we want to silence that inner play altogether. However, that voice, those images, and those feelings are tools that have helped humankind survive for millennia. They guided our ancestors to secure resources, avoid threats, and navigate complex social environments. This inner commentary, this intricate interplay of conscious and subconscious processes, is what we often refer to as the ego.

Yet the ego can become overbearing if left unchecked. As Robin Sharma aptly stated, *„The mind is a wonderful servant but a terrible master."* When it dominates, we may experience needless tension, stress, and conflict. A key source of this tension is the ego's strong dislike of cognitive dissonance: the discomfort that arises when reality does not match our internal expectations. Accepting that we are wrong can feel painful. To avoid that pain, the ego may fashion elaborate, sometimes absurd explanations or justifications to keep its version of reality intact. This can lead to stubbornness, denial, and a refusal to grow.

We've all witnessed situations where people hold tightly to beliefs that defy logic or evidence. They might staunchly defend these views, leaving us to wonder how they can be so convinced of something clearly untenable. Yet, this phenomenon affects everyone to some degree. Even the most rational among us have areas where we resist new information or interpret reality through a biased lens. This resistance is part of the ego's strategy to shield us from the existential discomfort of being wrong, maintaining our personal narrative as stable and coherent, at least from the inside. This resistance can escalate to extremes, as seen in certain psychological patterns that lock individuals into rigid self-narratives.

A particularly vivid example of this mechanism taken to an unhealthy extreme is seen in narcissistic individuals. It is often speculated that early childhood trauma, often within the first three years of life, triggers a hyper-protective ego structure. The narcissist's mind becomes rigid, rejecting any possibility of error to avoid cognitive dissonance at all costs. Their inner voice is never wrong in their own perception, and so they mold reality to fit their narrative. Others might find themselves ensnared in the narcissist's web, puzzled at how someone can believe such distorted truths.

Narcissists manage to keep the world at emotional bay by asserting their own „*truth*" aggressively. They seem to escape consequences because they deflect blame, shift narratives, and double down on their certainties. But this does not mean they are free of suffering. In fact, their life is marked by a constant state of war with the world and within themselves. Inner peace eludes them. No matter how powerful or respected they become, it never feels like enough. They cannot separate the internal voices from the observer, and thus, they have no capacity for genuine self-reflection. Without the ability to question their own path, they continue forward blindly. They are incapable of turning away from the edge of a metaphorical cliff, and their trajectory often ends in downfall, sometimes taking others with them.

When dealing with narcissists, it may be tempting to confront or attempt to correct them, yet doing so often fuels their insatiable need for attention. Engaging them on their terms means walking along their troubled path, giving them what they crave. To protect your own well-being, it can be wiser to step away, even if it feels unjust. Holding onto bitterness only harms you, as Ann Landers pointed out when she said that „*hanging onto resentment is letting someone you despise live rent-free in your head.*" Forgiving them isn't about excusing their actions; it's about releasing the emotional hold they have over you. By doing so, you free yourself from their narrative and reaffirm your place as an observer rather than a captive actor in their drama. In the words of Pyrrhus of Epirus, by holding onto it, you might „*Win the battle but lose the war.*"

In essence, this entire dynamic underscores the complexity of the human mind. This includes thinking in words, images, or feelings, toggling between the actor and observer roles, and grappling with the ego's resistance to pain and cognitive dissonance. By understanding that the voice in our head (the ego) is a survival tool rather than our true essence and by recognizing that an observer perspective is always available, we set the stage for a more harmonious inner experience. We learn that it is possible to watch the drama play out on the screen of our minds without always suffering as the lead character. We learn that forgiveness, not for the sake of others but for our own inner peace, liberates us from the burden of resentment.

All of this lays the groundwork for exploring the next crucial aspect of the ego: how it shapes our sense of self and identity. This inquiry will show that, beyond simply influencing our daily thoughts and feelings, the ego also contributes to the formation of our personal narratives and self-conceptions. Understanding this will be key as we move forward in examining why we hold onto certain beliefs, how we construct our identity, and why shedding some of these identifications can open the door to greater freedom, growth, and emotional resilience.

5.1 Observing the Ego

Having explored the interplay between the ego, the mind's inner dialogue, and the subtle shift from actor to observer in the previous section, we now turn to a crucial skill: observation. Observing the ego doesn't mean fighting it, shaming it, or attempting to annihilate it. Rather, it means learning to recognize the ego's patterns without judgment: its chatter, emotions, and impulses. This recognition helps us understand when the ego acts as a helpful guide and when it's running amok.

In some communities aware of the concept of ego, a misunderstanding often arises: they treat the ego as an inherently evil thing that must be destroyed. This perspective not only creates unnecessary guilt (after all, who wants to feel bad about something so intrinsic to their nature?), but it's also unrealistic. There is no human being without an ego. It's a fundamental aspect of our mind's architecture, a tool rather than a curse. The difference lies in how we use it. Ego, when properly understood, is like a compass or a weather vane. It gives us directional hints and information. Yet, we need not believe every reading at face value. The goal is not destruction but discernment.

By learning to observe the mind's chatter as if it were a passing stream of thoughts, we begin to differentiate between moments when the ego offers valuable insights and when it spins stories that cause stress, confusion, or unwarranted fear. This shift in perception is transformative. With consistent practice, you can listen to the voice in your head without immediately judging it, reacting to it, or mistaking it for your deepest self. Over time, this allows you to reanalyze your initial ego-driven assessments of situations. If your first interpretation was off the mark, you can correct it before it sets the tone for your entire emotional response. By repeatedly acknowledging, assessing, and recalibrating in this way, you gradually reshape your internal patterns.

This is one reason why meditative practices have been revered in numerous cultures for millennia. Meditation isn't about forcing the mind into silence; rather, it's about watching the mind work. You sit quietly, observe the flow of thoughts, and notice how they rise and fall, often without any intervention on your part. As you witness this process, the chatter naturally quiets. Without the relentless commentary, you free up psychic energy. You feel calmer, your focus sharpens, and you become more aware of the nuances in your internal landscape.

This observational skill becomes especially valuable in stressful or challenging situations. Under stress, the ego tries to interpret events based on familiar patterns. Sometimes, it provides a useful solution. Other times, it gets stuck, running in circles around a problem without finding a constructive way forward. When the ego is locked in such repetitive loops, it's often a sign of inner resistance.

Inner resistance can be thought of as psychological and emotional barriers within us that resist growth, change, and forward movement. It manifests as hesitation, fear, avoidance, or stubborn refusal to consider new perspectives. Often, this resistance stems from clinging to internal images or expectations about how reality should be rather than how it actually is. In these moments, the ego fights against reality, trying to force it to align with preconceived notions.

Recognizing when inner resistance arises and then learning how to deal with it is genuinely life-changing. The simplest way, when possible, is to take immediate action before the mind constructs an impenetrable wall of excuses. But what if you're already behind that wall, feeling stuck and overwhelmed?

In such cases, gently redirecting your attention to the immediate sensory world can help break the cycle. Notice your breathing pattern. Feel the touch of air against your skin. Listen to the sound of a distant bird or the hum of traffic outside. If you can, physically change your environment. A walk in the park, a short exercise session, or even just standing up and stretching can reset your inner state. Allow the mind's chatter to continue if it must, but refrain from pouring your attention into it. Keep returning to the present moment—the here and now—until the mental storm subsides. Once calmer, you can respond to the situation more rationally and effectively.

Your capacity to observe and manage your ego is influenced by three critical, interrelated factors:

1. **Physical Foundations:**
   The quality of your exercise, nutrition, and sleep affects your brain's physiology. When you're well-rested, nourished, and active, your mind is more resilient, flexible, and capable of nuanced thinking. Without proper self-care, even the best mental strategies falter.

2. **Memory and Emotional Charge:**
    Your past experiences, especially those wrapped
    in strong emotions, shape how you anticipate the
    future. If memories are heavily charged with
    anxiety or fear, your ego may become hyper-
    vigilant, interpreting new experiences as threats.
    By observing your inner responses, you recognize
    these patterns and eventually learn to release or
    reframe them.

3. **Environment and Social Influence:**
    We are social creatures. The people around us
    affect our mindset, goals, and beliefs. Your
    community, family, friends, and colleagues—each
    play a role in shaping your inner discourse. We
    often underestimate how much „our" ideas,
    aspirations, and judgments are actually borrowed
    from others. By observing these influences, we
    learn which external inputs serve us and which
    hinder our growth.

If any of these pillars is out of balance, for example, if
you're consistently sleep-deprived, your ego's chatter will
likely intensify and become less reliable. Poor sleep can
heighten emotions, trigger irrational fears, and make you
more reactive, which in turn affects your eating habits,
interactions with others, and overall mood. All three
factors are deeply interwoven. It's crucial to maintain a
healthy equilibrium to ensure the ego acts as a guide
rather than a tyrant.

As we observe our thoughts and examine how the ego
operates, it's important to understand one of its central
evolutionary purposes: keeping us safe within a group.
For our ancestors, being ostracized from the tribe meant

almost certain doom, due to scarce resources, vulnerability to predators, or even lethal hostility from former companions. Thus, conforming to group beliefs, norms, and goals was a matter of survival. Over thousands of years, the ego adapted to priorities, fitting in, and adopting the values and behaviors of the tribe.

Today, this survival mechanism still influences us. We now live in large, complex societies, and yet our ego still nudges us to align with a group's expectations. We often remain painfully unaware of how much of our internal chatter and decision-making processes are guided by the implicit rules and ideologies of our chosen communities. We rarely question the beliefs handed down to us, be they cultural, political, or even spiritual. Just as we trust our parents' warning that fire burns without verifying it personally, we trust countless other notions we've never examined closely.

It's easy to look back at history and recognize harmful ideologies and outdated beliefs that led to suffering or injustice. But we are less inclined to examine our current beliefs with the same rigor. Yet, if we truly want to grow, we must apply the observer's lens to our own era, our own circles, and our own minds.

Part of this self-examination includes acknowledging the profound influence our social circle has on us. One well-known maxim states, *„You're the average of the five people you spend the most time with."* The people closest to us shape our worldview, our aspirations, and even our sense of self-worth. To change your goals, beliefs, or personal trajectory, you may need to reevaluate the company you keep. This doesn't mean callously discarding long-time friends, but it does mean recognizing whether your environment supports your growth or holds you back.

If you surround yourself with individuals who challenge you in a healthy way, inspire you, and foster positive habits, then you're setting the stage for meaningful development. Conversely, if those around you encourage destructive patterns, reinforce limiting beliefs, or constantly immerse you in drama, your ego will echo those influences, making it harder to evolve into the person you want to be.

As you apply these observational skills, you'll find it easier to engage with the world authentically. Over time, the line between „inner" and „outer" quiets down. You begin to realize that much of what you assumed was an intrinsic part of your identity or personality is actually fluid. It's shaped by your environment, physical health, and social input. Equipped with this understanding, you can move forward to the next dimensions of self-exploration. We will examine how identity is formed, how attachment to certain labels limits your experience, and how to cultivate a more unified sense of being in the upcoming sections.

5.2 Transforming insecurity to safety

In previous sections, we explored the complexity of the ego, the importance of observing our internal landscape, and the interplay between our personal identity and the world around us. These insights set the stage for another crucial dimension of human experience: safety, both real and perceived. By understanding how the ego influences our sense of security, we can begin to master our own inner responses, freeing ourselves from patterns of fear that limit our growth. To understand this, we must first explore how our perceptions of safety often diverge from reality itself.

A key idea here is that the feeling of safety does not always align with objective reality. Consider the free climber, scaling a sheer cliff face without ropes. Objectively, they are in great danger. One misstep could be fatal. Yet if this climber trusts their skills, training, and experience, they may feel completely at ease. On the other hand, a person sitting comfortably in an airplane, one of the safest forms of transportation, might feel terrified. Their nervous system, influenced by mental images of calamity or entrenched beliefs about flying, reacts as though they are in imminent peril. This disconnect reveals that fear and safety are not dictated solely by facts but also by our perception and interpretation of those facts.

Our sense of safety is deeply intertwined with what we believe about the world. If we trust that the metal tube flying through the sky is engineered for reliability and that the pilots are well-trained professionals, we can relax and enjoy the flight. If we do not hold that belief, we remain tense despite clear statistics showing the low risk of air travel. This underscores a fundamental truth: the mind's perception often holds more sway over our emotional state than objective circumstances do.

Our tendency to feel unsafe even when we are relatively secure is rooted in our evolutionary history. Humans evolved in environments where threats were immediate and real, such as hungry predators, hostile neighbors, and scarce resources. The nervous system adapted to detect danger quickly and trigger fight-or-flight responses, mobilizing the body for survival. This was an invaluable trait in the wild, ensuring that when a threat appeared, we reacted without delay. Those who paused to ponder the facts rather than reacting swiftly were less likely to pass their genes forward.

Today, we inhabit a globalized, interconnected world where actual physical threats are often far less frequent than our ancestors faced. We interact with strangers from across the planet, collaborate in workplaces filled with diverse individuals, and navigate busy cities without constant mortal peril. Yet our nervous system still carries the old wiring, ready to sound alarms at a moment's notice. This can lead to chronic anxiety, stress, and tension, especially if we have not developed the skills to discern between a genuinely dangerous situation and a benign one that merely feels scary because it's unfamiliar.

If we rely on logic alone, telling ourselves, „You're safe,“ rarely makes deep fear disappear instantly. Fear, anxiety, and panic arise faster than rational thought can intervene. When we experience turbulence on a plane or walk down a dark street late at night, our racing heartbeat and shallow breathing tell us that our body believes we're in danger. Yet logically, we know that nothing is likely to harm us.

To break these patterns, we need to become present with our fear. Instead of fleeing from discomfort or trying to argue it out of existence, we can allow ourselves to feel it fully. This practice involves staying with the sensation of fear long enough to observe it as it is: a set of bodily sensations and mental associations that, while unpleasant, are not truly lethal. As we do this, tension begins to release, the breath deepens, and the nervous system finds its way back to equilibrium. This approach mirrors the methods discussed in previous sections, including observation without judgment, being in the present moment, and questioning old narratives.

Meditation provides an excellent training ground for this skill. By sitting still without flinching, we confront whatever arises, be it physical discomfort, anxious thoughts, or restlessness. Over time, we learn that these states come and go. They are transient, not permanent. This insight gradually reconditions our nervous system, showing us that we can endure feelings of insecurity without losing control. As fear dissipates, or at least becomes more manageable, we discover that feeling safe is not entirely dependent on external conditions. It can be cultivated from within.

Learning to feel safe in uncomfortable or uncertain conditions unlocks a profound sense of freedom. Instead of being prisoners of our instincts, we become conscious actors capable of responding thoughtfully to challenges. When you know how to access a sense of inner security, you can step into new situations with confidence and openness, whether that means meeting new people, taking on a new job, or exploring unfamiliar environments. This adaptability and willingness to engage with the unknown increases your value in relationships, communities, and professional settings. It makes you a more resilient, flexible individual who is not easily swayed by the winds of uncertainty.

Moreover, this newfound inner stability paves the way for deep personal growth. When your decisions are not governed by automatic fear responses, you have room to question old beliefs, update your assumptions about the world, and refine your goals. You can rely less on inherited ideologies or the anxiety-driven need to conform and more on your developing wisdom and empathy.

It might seem paradoxical that the best way to gain control over fear is to release the need for immediate control. Yet this is precisely what sitting with fear teaches us. By not fleeing discomfort, we learn that fear cannot hold us hostage unless we allow it. Instead of tightening our grip, we loosen it. Observing fear's rise and fall without resistance. Over time, this practice transforms our relationship with fear itself. We no longer see it as a permanent, oppressive force but rather as a passing state of mind and body, one that we can acknowledge and outlast.

This ability to feel safe, even when confronted by unsettling scenarios, expands our freedom. Without exaggerated fear, the world feels more accessible, people seem more approachable, and opportunities more plentiful. The ego, instead of being a reactive mechanism locked in survival mode, can begin serving its more noble purpose, which is connecting conscious awareness with the subconscious storehouse of knowledge and intuition, guiding us toward a richer, more fulfilling experience of life.

This exploration of safety complements what we've uncovered in earlier sections about identity, observation, and the ego's influence. Just as identifying too strongly with internal labels or trusting the ego's chatter can limit us, clinging to a distorted sense of danger can trap us in a narrow comfort zone. By recognizing that safety is as much an internal creation as an external condition, we align ourselves with the overarching theme of these discussions: liberation through understanding.

In upcoming sections, we will delve deeper into how our identity and belief structures, as well as logical fallacies and cognitive biases, influence our perception of reality. Just as learning to observe the ego helps us understand our internal chatter, learning to distinguish between true threats and imagined dangers refines our ability to move gracefully through the world. Overcoming fear is not about eliminating risk. Life will always have its uncertainties. Rather, it's about transforming our response so that fear no longer paralyzes us. This internal freedom allows us to engage more meaningfully with life's challenges, to grow from our experiences, and to ultimately construct a more stable, open, and authentic version of ourselves.

5.3 The Ego's Tricks

In the previous sections, we delved into how the ego shapes our sense of identity, influences how we observe our thoughts, and affects our perception of safety. We've seen that the ego is not merely a villain to be vanquished but a tool that, when understood, can foster resilience, peace, and personal growth. Yet, to fully appreciate the scope of the ego's influence, we must also examine how our beliefs intersect with our sense of self. These beliefs are often upheld and defended by subtle mental maneuvers. In other words, understanding the ego's role in our cognitive landscape also involves shining a light on the ways we trick ourselves and others, often without even realizing it. Central to these maneuvers are the beliefs we hold, which shape our reality more than we often realize.

Beliefs act as the scaffolding upon which we build our reality. They guide our decisions, influence our emotional states, and determine how we interpret the world's events. But there's an important distinction between holding a belief and requiring its validation from reality. As Terence McKenna famously said: „Belief is a toxic and dangerous attitude toward reality. After all, if it's there, it doesn't require your belief—and if it's not there, why should you believe in it?" This quote challenges us to examine how often we accept ideas without evidence. Such unexamined beliefs can lock us into rigid identities and limit our capacity for growth. When the ego is at the helm, protecting these beliefs becomes a matter of preserving our self-image. We cling to them not necessarily because they are true but because admitting they might be false would create cognitive dissonance. This is where the sunk cost fallacy often creeps in: we stick to a belief because we've invested time, energy, or emotion in it, even when evidence suggests it's time to let go. Worse, the backfire effect can make us cling tighter when faced with contradictory facts, as the ego doubles down to shield itself.

Yet, you are not obligated to hold an opinion on matters for which you have no evidence. Learning to say „I don't know" or „I have no opinion yet" relieves the ego of the burden of defending a stance built on shaky ground. This counters the confirmation bias that drives us to seek only what supports our views, ignoring what doesn't, and the self-serving bias, where we attribute successes to our own brilliance but failures to outside forces. This creates a more open, flexible mindset, one that allows you to learn from new experiences, integrate fresh insights, and refine your worldview as evidence presents itself.

Our inner monologue often employs the same logical shortcuts and distortions that appear in external debates. The ego uses these mental maneuvers, known as logical fallacies and cognitive biases, to shield cherished beliefs from scrutiny. While the ego's original intent might be self-protection, these distortions ultimately undermine our ability to see clearly and adjust when necessary. Two prime examples are the „sunk cost fallacy" and the „backfire effect," which we've already touched on. But it doesn't stop there. In our minds or conversations, we might dismiss a challenge with an ad hominem attack, asking „Who are you to judge?" rather than engaging the argument. Or we might build a straw man, misrepresenting an opposing view to knock it down more easily. These tricks are subtle but pervasive, shaping how we defend our sense of self.

Instead, consider how the Dunning-Kruger effect plays a role: when we know little, we often overestimate our competence, while deeper understanding brings humility. By recognizing these patterns, such as the sunk cost fallacy, backfire effect, confirmation bias, self-serving bias, ad hominem, straw man, and Dunning-Kruger effect, we can pause before passing judgment or clinging to outdated beliefs. These are just a sample of the ego's distortions, but they highlight how it warps reality to protect itself.

The ego's toolkit of distortions stretches far beyond what we've explored here. These examples are merely a starting point, a peek into the countless ways our minds bend reality to preserve our sense of self. For those eager to dig deeper, resources like The Skeptic's Guide to the Universe by Steven Novella or online compilations of logical fallacies and cognitive biases catalog hundreds of these mental traps. Each is a subtle snare set by the ego. Spotting even a handful begins to unravel its illusions, prompting us to question what we cling to and why.

By understanding these fallacies and biases, we become better equipped to identify when our ego defends its worldview unfairly. Recognizing the ego's tricks helps us pause before passing judgment, making snap decisions, or clinging to outmoded beliefs. It helps us remain open-minded, questioning our assumptions and embracing uncertainty where appropriate.

Embracing the possibility that our beliefs might be incorrect can feel unsettling. Yet this openness is the pathway to intellectual freedom and personal growth. When we allow ourselves to have no opinion on matters lacking evidence, we free up mental space that would otherwise be occupied by rigid stances. This doesn't mean becoming apathetic; rather, it means staying curious and responsive. We remain flexible ready to update our views as we learn more.

This attitude aligns perfectly with the observational perspective we've discussed before. Just as we can observe our inner chatter without judgment, we can also observe our beliefs and attachments. When we see that certain identities, ideologies, or viewpoints cause unnecessary suffering, we can gently loosen our grip. Instead of forcing the world to match our internal assumptions, we adapt to the world as it is. This reduces inner resistance, mitigating the emotional turmoil from forcing square pegs into round holes.

Ultimately, learning to feel safe is about reclaiming control over your internal state. When you can feel secure regardless of external circumstances, you unlock a profound sense of freedom. You're no longer governed by automatic reactions based on old fears. Instead, you operate from a place of strength and groundedness, allowing your true potential to emerge. By mastering the skill of feeling safe, you pave the way for deeper personal development and a life lived from a place of peace rather than fear.

We've already seen how ego, identity, observation, and safety interrelate with belief. Now, with an expanded toolbox of critical thinking skills and a clearer map of our inner fallacies, we are positioned to navigate life's challenges with greater discernment. Understanding these cognitive and emotional dynamics lays the groundwork for becoming the calm, centered observer who can engage with the world intelligently, compassionately, and authentically. Free from the illusions that once held us back.

5.4 Integration and Practical Application: Living with a Balanced Ego

Having explored how the ego forms our identity, shapes our thought patterns, influences our sense of safety, and safeguards our beliefs, we now stand at a point of integration. We've seen how observation without judgment can calm our inner dialogue, how understanding the difference between feeling safe and actually being safe can free us from irrational fears, and how recognizing logical fallacies and cognitive biases can prevent our ego from tricking us into clinging to outdated assumptions. The question now is: how do we bring all these insights together to improve our everyday lives?

First, it's crucial to reaffirm that the ego is not an enemy. Neither is it something to be destroyed or suppressed. Rather, the ego is a complex, ancient tool that has guided human beings through millennia of survival challenges. Its patterns, such as forming attachments, avoiding cognitive dissonance, seeking safety, and aligning with social norms, once served as life-saving instincts. Now, as we navigate a modern world rich with information and complexity, these same tendencies can become limiting if we don't observe and adjust them consciously.

By viewing the ego as a functional ally, we learn to appreciate its strengths. It helps us pick up social cues, stay vigilant when necessary, and form a coherent sense of self. Yet, we must also recognize when the ego oversteps its bounds, when it holds onto harmful beliefs, locks us into unhelpful identities, or stokes unnecessary fears. The path forward involves balancing respect for the ego's evolutionary purpose with a commitment to mastering its influence.

Changing our relationship with the ego starts by refining our inner narrative. By paying attention to our internal chatter, whether it comes as words, images, or feelings, we gain a clear view of how our ego constructs meaning. We notice when we label ourselves with traits that limit our potential: „*I'm just not good at that,*" „*I always fail when I try something new,*" or „*I can't trust anyone.*" These thought patterns form an identity that can become self-fulfilling.

However, when we step back into the observer's role, we can question these labels. Is it truly impossible for us to acquire new skills, or are we using past difficulties to excuse future efforts? Are we genuinely incapable of forming trust, or have we allowed one or two betrayals to shape a universal belief? By catching such narratives as they arise, we can dismantle them. This frees us to adopt more accurate, growth-oriented self-perceptions: „*I can learn over time,*" „*I've had some setbacks, but I can adapt,*" or „*I might have to be cautious, but I can still connect with others meaningfully.*"

As we refine our internal narrative, we become better equipped to handle challenging emotions. Fear, anxiety, loneliness, and anger are all states the ego seeks to either avoid or justify. Without observation and reflection, these emotions can spiral into larger-than-life problems. By practicing stillness through techniques such as meditation or even mindful moments during the day, we learn to tolerate discomfort. Instead of panicking when fear arises, we allow ourselves to feel it fully, notice it pass, and then act from a calmer space.

This emotional flexibility doesn't mean we never experience negative feelings. Rather, it ensures that when these emotions arise, they do not overwhelm our decision-making capacity. We recognize them as signals rather than definitive truths. A moment of fear might mean we need to assess risk more carefully, not that we must avoid the situation altogether. A bout of loneliness might signal we need more meaningful connections, not that we are doomed to isolation.

Confronting our beliefs with honesty and humility is another integral step. We've learned that the ego often fears admitting it's wrong due to the pain of cognitive dissonance. But acknowledging that a belief no longer serves us, whether it's about our abilities, other people, or the way the world works, is an act of courage that leads to growth.

When we find ourselves resisting new information or doubling down in the face of contradictory evidence, that's a cue to pause. Ask: „*What am I protecting here? Is it my self-image, my pride, or a sense of certainty that feels comforting?*" As we become willing to let go of unverified assumptions, we cultivate a mental environment where learning and adaptation thrive. Over time, this openness to new data, perspectives, and experiences makes us more capable of thriving in a rapidly changing world.

Our social environment plays a profound role in reinforcing or challenging our ego's narratives. Surrounding ourselves with people who encourage curiosity, critical thinking, empathy, and personal growth can reinforce the healthier patterns we are trying to establish. Conversely, consistently immersing ourselves in groups that demand conformity, ignore evidence, or applaud destructive behaviors will strengthen the ego's resistance to change.

This does not mean we must abandon old friends or family ties, but we should be aware of the subtle influences they have on us. Where possible, engage with communities, mentors, and peers who embody the qualities you want to cultivate in yourself. If you seek to be more open-minded, spend time with those who listen attentively and evaluate ideas based on merit. If you hope to be more empathetic and less judgmental, surround yourself with people who demonstrate kindness and understanding.

Practical Techniques for Day-to-Day Life:

- **Mindful Check-Ins:** Throughout the day, pause and notice your internal state. Are you caught in a loop of negative self-talk or worry? Take a moment to observe these thoughts without attaching to them. A few deep breaths and a reminder that you are the observer, not the actor trapped in the drama, can be transformative.

- **Journaling:** Write down your recurring beliefs about yourself and the world. Look for patterns. Are they based on evidence or assumptions? Are they serving your growth or holding you back? Journaling provides a concrete record of your internal landscape, making it easier to spot fallacies and biases.

- **Gradual Exposure to Discomfort:** Safely expose yourself to situations that feel intimidating, knowing you can rely on the observation skills you've developed. Over time, this rewires your nervous system to handle uncertainty and fear without panic.

- **Questioning Group Norms:** Pay attention to groupthink or in-group bias. Ask yourself why you hold certain collective beliefs. Is it because they are true or simply because they are popular in your social circle?

- **Celebrate Openness:** When you find yourself admitting uncertainty or accepting a correction, acknowledge it as a victory. This willingness to update your worldview is evidence of a flexible, maturing ego.

Throughout these chapters, we've touched on the ego's origins, its protective functions, its tricky maneuvers, and the limitations it imposes when unexamined. We've seen how observation, balance, critical thinking, and mindful presence can transform what might initially seem like an internal adversary into a cooperative partner on our life's journey.

This integration, allowing the ego to serve rather than dominate, is not a one-time task. It's an ongoing process of learning, adjusting, and evolving. You may find that certain beliefs or fears reemerge under stress or that, as your life circumstances change, new identities and attachments form. Each time, the tools of mindful observation, logical scrutiny, emotional regulation, and open-minded curiosity will help you navigate these shifts with greater ease and grace.

6 Time
Embracing the Eternal Now

Our perception of time fundamentally shapes our experience of life. By focusing on the present rather than becoming trapped in regrets of the past or fears of the future, we can reclaim joy and meaning. This idea isn't just a theoretical concept. It has been lived out by remarkable individuals who have found serenity even in the most chaotic of circumstances.

Take Thích Nhất Hạnh, a Zen Buddhist monk whose life was forged in the crucible of the Vietnam War. Born in 1926, he grew up in a world that was rapidly changing, and by the time war broke out, his homeland was torn apart by violence, loss, and suffering. As bombs fell and villages burned, it would have been easy to succumb to despair or anger. Yet Nhất Hạnh chose a different path.

Walking through the wreckage of war-torn villages, he did something extraordinary: he focused on his steps. Slowly, deliberately, he practiced what he called walking meditation. Each step was taken with full attention, each breath a moment of calm amidst the chaos. „When we walk," he would later say, „we arrive with every step." It wasn't a means of escape; it was a way to remain fully present in a world that demanded his presence. Picture it: bombs echoing in the distance, yet here's a man finding peace in the rhythm of his own feet. How's that for a rebellion against chaos?

His practice was transformative for those around him. While others were consumed by the fear of what might come next, Nhất Hạnh found strength in anchoring himself to the now. He often taught that mindfulness wasn't just for the peaceful moments in life. It was a skill to carry into the storms. Even amid unimaginable suffering, he showed that the present moment could be a sanctuary.

Nhất Hạnh's teachings remind us that we don't need perfect conditions to access the power of the present or to glimpse the stillness of Satori. The beauty of life isn't found in the past we can't change or the future we can't predict. It's here, right now, in the simplest acts of being alive. His life serves as a testament to the idea that no matter how chaotic the world around us becomes, there is always a way to reclaim peace within ourselves.

6.1 The Mind's Time Trap

Our memories not only shape our understanding of the past but also influence our predictions for the future. The evolutionary advantage of memory lies in its ability to recognize patterns, helping us predict potential future events based on past experiences. A rustle in the bushes might signal a snake or a bunny or, if you're particularly unlucky, a snake *holding* a bunny, requiring different levels of alertness. Yet, in today's world, this once-vital system often struggles to keep pace with the complexities of modern life.

While memory evolved as a survival mechanism, helping our ancestors escape immediate dangers, modern life overwhelms this system. The threats we face today are not life-or-death encounters but relentless demands: deadlines, exams, and societal expectations. Unlike the temporary nature of past dangers, modern stress is chronic, leaving us stuck in a state of mental overdrive. Instead of running away from a bear occasionally, ever since we became sedentary, we have to constantly perform in our workplace or school. Yet we miss a tribe with whom we could share our adventure of escaping a fatal encounter with destiny, and the calming effects of a natural environment are not available as well. This brings us to a conundrum of the comfortable life that culture and civilization have brought forth. Our mind is constantly working to make sense of the world. But the world is there to be experienced, not to make sense of.

René Descartes famously said, „*I think, therefore I am,*" but this perspective may oversimplify the nature of our existence. Thinking is just one facet of consciousness. A survival tool rather than the essence of who we are. The real beauty of life lies in our capacity to experience and explore it. Meaning and purpose are human constructs designed to flatter the ego and serve societal expectations. You don't need a grand purpose to justify your existence. Your purpose is simply to live fully. Would you demand a flower explain its purpose? Like a flower, a rabbit, or a fish, you don't need a reason to exist. Clinging to the idea of a „*higher purpose*" can become a trap, stealing the freedom to embrace life as it is: precious, fleeting, and inherently enough. What if, just for a moment, you dropped the „why" and felt the „is"?

This tension between doing and being reveals a deeper truth about our existence. Doing keeps us tethered to the future, always striving for the next goal, the next validation, the next escape from stress. It's a restless state, one that fuels mental overdrive and disconnects us from the present. In contrast, being anchors us in the now, where life simply unfolds. There is no effort, no control, just presence. This state of being aligns with what Zen traditions call Satori, unburdened by the need to achieve or understand. Satori isn't a destination to reach through doing; it's a recognition of what already is when we let go of striving.

Imagine living like that flower or rabbit: not defined by what you accomplish but by the simple fact of your presence. In Satori, there's no pressure to perform, no demand for purpose beyond the act of being. It's a shift from stress to flow, from effort to effortlessness, where the mind quiets and the world reveals itself as it is. Our journey isn't about escaping the modern conundrum through more doing, more tasks or more fixes, but about surrendering to being, stepping into the stillness that Satori promises. Here, you're not what you think or achieve; you're the awareness that experiences life fully, moment by moment, free from the traps of memory or expectation. What would it feel like to let go, right this second?

6.3 Reclaiming the Moment

Envision yourself stepping onto an old pier, its weathered boards creaking under your bare feet as you wander toward the edge. You came here to think about the job teetering on the edge, the argument still buzzing in your skull, the bills stacking up like a storm ready to break. But as you reach the end, something shifts. The water laps gently against the posts below, a soft rhythm that doesn't care about your worries. A breeze tugs at your hair, carrying the scent of pine and damp earth, and for no reason at all, you stop. Really stop. Not to plan, not to fix, just to stand there.

You notice the sunlight fracturing across the lake's surface, a thousand tiny mirrors dancing without purpose. A fish breaks the stillness, sending ripples outward, and you watch them spread, then fade, as if the water's already let go. Your breath slows, falling into step with the rise and fall of the waves, and that knot in your chest loosens, not because anything's changed, but because you're not fighting it anymore. The future, with its deadlines and demands, drifts away, like a radio station you've turned down. The past, with its jagged edges, blurs into something you don't need to grip so tightly.

A dragonfly zips by, its iridescent wings catching the light, and a laugh slips out of you. A small, unplanned sound that catches you off guard. You don't need to know where it's headed or why it's here. It just is, and so are you. The pier, the lake, the sky are not waiting for you to figure them out. They simply exist, and right now, so do you, weightless and whole, as if time's hit pause just to let you be. Later, you'll walk back to your car, back to the hum of life, but at this moment, standing here, you're not just in it. You are it, alive, unscripted, and enough. This is Satori, the quiet arrival into what already is. This fleeting moment of presence raises a deeper question about what truly matters across the vast expanse of time.

Whether your worldview is religious, scientific, or spiritual, one question remains universal: Do our actions truly matter in the grand scheme of time? History shows that even the most iconic figures like Newton and Caesar will eventually fade from memory. This realization does not need to plunge us into nihilism but should inspire us to embrace life fully, untethered from the need to leave a legacy. After all, the grates probably never worried about their TikTok engagement.

If striving for the future feels futile, can we at least trust our past? Surprisingly, the answer is often no. Memory is less a perfect recording and more a reconstruction shaped by emotions and personal narratives. For example, witnesses in court frequently provide conflicting or inaccurate accounts, as stress and the passage of time distort their recollections. Memory is less a recording and more like that friend who embellishes every story. It's exciting to listen to, but not entirely trustworthy.

Emotional memories, while deeply impactful, are particularly prone to this distortion, often influencing our sense of self and shaping our identity based on incomplete or skewed perspectives. This highlights an important truth: while the past informs who we are, it is not an unchangeable script. Our memories are tools to guide us, but they are not infallible, and understanding their fluid nature can help us approach both the past and present with greater mindfulness.

Try this exercise: Recall your most cherished memory. Close your eyes and immerse yourself in the emotions it evokes. Now, what is it that you noticed? Was the emotion still sweet in the end, or did it become bittersweet? There is no need to do the same exercise with an already bitter memory. But it is essential to notice that every emotionally charged memory of the past will turn bitter. The same is true for any hopes for the future. A study by Cornell University concluded that 85% of all worries will not happen, and of the 15% that will happen, 79% were surprisingly easily handled. Seneca described it as follows: „*We suffer more often in the imagination than in reality.*"Yet, these 97% of meaningless thoughts cause stress and adverse health effects.

Realizing that thoughts of the future and past are often meaningless can leave a bitter taste of nihilism. However, while life may have no inherent meaning beyond what we give it, there is a purpose: to experience your journey to the fullest. You don't ask a tiger or a tree for meaning, yet they thrive in nature, fighting for their right to exist. This realization should shift your focus from searching for meaning to fully experiencing life. How deeply can you dive into each moment? We shift from „*why to live*" to

„how to live". Whenever we are fully present, we are blissful. Quoting Eckhart Tolle, *„Time isn't precious at all because it is an illusion. What you perceive as precious is not time but the one point that is out of time: the Now. That is precious indeed. The more you are focused on time—past and future—the more you miss the Now, the most precious thing there is."*

As everyone has experienced a flow state and its timeless beauty, it is a good way to describe what Eckhart Tolle tries to describe in his book 'The Power of Now'. But imagine instead of being in a challenging game, you can access this state even in a mundane situation, like folding laundry or being stuck in traffic. That's Satori peeking through the ordinary. In my personal experience, even then, you may find yourself drawn back into the cycle of what was and will be. Constant bliss wasn't ideal for survival. Imagine a caveman so blissed out he didn't notice the tiger about to make him lunch. At this point, I believe that our natural state is one of bliss, and our instinct for survival, e.g., the ego, must suppress this feeling to prevent us from getting eaten by a tiger or our boss. Despite some spiritual teachers viewing the ego as a hindrance, I see it as a natural and necessary aspect of our existence.

Our suffering often stems from the mind's fixation on the past or future, pulling us away from the richness of the present. While planning and reflecting are valuable, they should serve as tools, not traps. By understanding how to let go of emotionally charged memories and unproductive worries, we can free ourselves to fully embrace the now. The only place where life truly unfolds. The same distinction applies to being anxious about the future versus planning for it. The difference lies in the emotional charge. When accessing the wisdom of our past or planning the future, there is no emotional charge. But unresolved emotions that we haven't let go of add an emotional charge to memories.

It is worth noting that anxious thoughts of the future are also based on our memory, particularly memories of our past behavior. With our actions, we build evidence for who we are. If we have enough evidence that we will do what we say we will, we reduce our anxieties about future events. If we have successfully mastered enough negative experiences in the past, we trust that we will handle them in the future as well. This is crucial in child development, as while we want to help others, especially those related to us, doing so can deprive them of opportunities to build their self-esteem. Growth usually happens when we must overcome difficulties.

Facing new events, especially those extremely foreign to our understanding of reality, can lead to biases, as our minds rely on outdated information. It is like trying to navigate with an ancient map that says, 'Here be dragons.' Spoiler alert: no dragons, just Wi-Fi dead zones. Mindfulness, including being aware of our thoughts, can help us avoid such misunderstandings and stay present in the moment.

7 Limiting Beliefs
Breaking Free from Mental Barriers

It all starts with your beliefs, those invisible glasses through which you view the world. And let's be honest, some of us are wearing lenses smudged with self-doubt and pessimism. It might not come as a surprise that your experience of life is greatly influenced by your beliefs. Yet, many of us hesitate to challenge these deeply held beliefs. Before we can change our lives, we must change what we believe is possible.

To achieve your dreams, you must first believe in their possibility. Imagine if Harrison Ford had told George Lucas, 'I'm not good enough to be Han Solo.' We'd probably have a stormtrooper accidentally piloting the

Millennium Falcon. Instead, he dared to believe in himself, embracing the opportunity despite his lack of experience, and the rest is history.

Limiting beliefs are self-imposed perceptions that restrict our potential and choices. Often rooted in past experiences or distorted perceptions, they act as psychological barriers, convincing us we're incapable or unworthy of success. Telling oneself, „I'm not good enough,“ „I'll never succeed,“ or „People like me can't achieve that,“ undermines self-confidence, perpetuates self-doubt, and prevents personal growth. These beliefs cause us to unconsciously limit ourselves and our possibilities in life. Along this journey, it is important to recognize when we have such beliefs, as they will hinder us from becoming who we want to be.

Marcus Aurelius once said, „If something is humanly possible, it is attainable by you too.“ The first person who must believe in you is yourself. View the world as a playground and determine what steps you need to take to reach your desired destination, and you will find yourself on a different adventure. Your beliefs about the world influence your perception of it. If your perception of the world changes, so will your experience of it. Therefore, changing your beliefs will change your experience of the world.

7.1 Identifying and Challenging Limiting Beliefs

To change your beliefs, you must first notice the ones that hold you back. The reason we are often unaware of our limiting patterns is that our minds rationalize them. Our mind is a master at justifying any behavior we display. In this book, you will learn how to observe yourself better and improve your awareness.

Once you identify a limiting belief, accept it, but still take action. This creates new evidence for you to form new, empowering beliefs. This journey is not comfortable. For most people, their current comfort zone is a prison. For some, even depression can become a comfort zone, and while breaking out of it is necessary, the world outside can seem scarier than repeating familiar patterns.

Consider the story of Srinivasa Ramanujan, a self-taught mathematical genius from India. Despite having no formal training and facing immense skepticism from the academic community, Ramanujan believed in his abilities and persisted. He sent his groundbreaking work to G.H. Hardy, a prominent mathematician at Cambridge, who recognized his genius and invited him to England. Ramanujan's belief in his potential, despite numerous obstacles, allowed him to contribute significantly to mathematics and leave a lasting legacy.

7.2 Practical Steps to Overcome Limiting Beliefs

Visualization is a powerful tool for transforming beliefs. For instance, if approaching your crush feels daunting, picture yourself doing it successfully. To enhance this practice, visualize during moments of calm, such as in the morning or after meditation. How you visualize is up to you. The key is to fully immerse yourself in the imagined scenario, experiencing it as though it's happening right now. Athletes often visualize their moves before executing them. The only rule about visualization is that you must feel as if it is happening to you right now. Feel the emotions, see the colors, and experience it with all your senses. This is the first step to convincing yourself that it is possible. Yet, to turn this vision into reality, you must pair imagination with tangible steps forward.

The second step is to take action. Visualization alone is not enough; it must be accompanied by concrete steps toward your goal. By consistently taking action, you create new experiences and evidence that reinforce your new, empowering beliefs. Let's be real: visualizing yourself talking to your crush isn't going to make them suddenly appear at your door with flowers. But hey, it might save you from a few awkward stutters. The real question is, who do you need to become for your crush to be with you? What actions must you take to achieve your worldly desires? Next, consider whether these changes align with your true self.

We are capable of dramatic change, but we might not always be happy with the result. Sometimes, the world rejecting our demands is the best thing that can happen to us. Whatever happens in the process, always assume it is for your growth as a person. You don't develop patience by always getting immediate gratification, nor do you become resilient without facing challenges. It is these challenges in life that shape us into who we are today. The only promise I can give is that by becoming the best version of yourself, you will live an astonishing life.

7.3 Navigating Paradoxical Beliefs

Limiting beliefs aren't just personal. They can also be society's way of handing you a poorly written user manual for life. For example, the belief that free will is an illusion, though philosophically intriguing, can hinder growth by diminishing our sense of agency. This idea can be unsettling, as it implies we have no real control over our lives. While determinism is a fascinating and complex topic, it can be more restrictive than liberating in practical terms. If the world truly is deterministic and all choices are preordained, that doesn't erase the significance of our actions; instead, it underscores the importance of each „*choice*" in defining an inevitable historical path. Even if free will is an illusion, our actions still carry weight. So, shouldn't we approach each decision as if it were genuinely ours to make, acting thoughtfully and responsibly?

One might argue that if the world is deterministic, our decisions are irrelevant. Why strive if everything is predestined? In this view, even a murderer's actions were inevitable, each step in their life leading inexorably to their „*decision*" to take another's life. Yet, for society to function and to deter future crimes, we must operate as though people have agency. This means holding individuals accountable as if their choices were indeed their own. So, despite any personal belief in determinism, we must, for all practical purposes, act as though free will exists. This approach helps foster accountability and supports a constructive path forward for everyone. Beyond such abstract debates, our beliefs about others can also create barriers that limit both personal growth and societal harmony.

While the previous paradox seems easy to digest, it will become harder the more we identify with the belief. Beliefs about social issues can unintentionally limit your potential and even deepen social divides. For instance, if you believe that certain groups are actively blocking your success, you may feel justified in adopting an „us vs. them" mindset, which fuels resentment and reinforces division. This belief can trap you in a cycle of blame, where energy that could be used productively is instead spent on perceived obstacles.

Ironically, by seeing others as „the enemy," you risk becoming rigid in your approach, only strengthening the biases you initially wanted to overcome. If you are going into a conflict, you are validating that the characteristic discriminated against matters. True progress comes not from resisting others' views but from focusing on your own goals, forming connections across differences, and proving that success can transcend social boundaries. By letting go of limiting beliefs about others, you empower yourself to move forward authentically, becoming a bridge rather than a barrier in society. You will become an example that the characteristic never mattered, to begin with.

Daryl Davis, a Black musician, defied limiting beliefs about division and conflict by engaging directly with KKK members. Through curiosity and respect, he opened dialogues that dismantled stereotypes, ultimately inspiring over 200 members to leave the Klan. His story shows the transformative power of letting go of the belief that 'us vs. them' is inevitable. If Davis had approached them with overt hostility or treated their beliefs as barriers, he might have reinforced the divide, validating their prejudices. Instead, he showed that connection, even across deep-seated divides, can dissolve hate and foster understanding. Davis's story illustrates the power of letting go of the belief that „*us vs. them*" is inevitable; by connecting authentically, he catalyzed meaningful change without compromising his values.

8 Awareness
Reclaiming the Present

Awareness is crucial not only for letting go of what doesn't serve us but also for enriching our life experience. Consider walking along a beautiful road for the very first time. At the start, you are in awe: the vibrant flowers draw your eye, the intricate designs on the buildings captivate you, and the unique patterns of the cobblestones intrigue you. Each step brings fresh wonder and delight. However, over time, the novelty fades. The road itself remains unchanged, yet your perception becomes dulled by familiarity. The first time you were fully engaged, your senses heightened. The next time, you might still notice the flowers and feel a brief moment of bliss, but your mind quickly becomes preoccupied with other thoughts. Eventually, what was once a captivating route becomes just another street fulfilling its basic function. The difference in these experiences has nothing to do with the road. It stems entirely from your level of awareness. Yet, this loss of wonder is not permanent, as a simple shift in focus can revive the magic of that first encounter.

Occasionally, a memory of your initial delight resurfaces. You recall how much you once loved walking along this very path. By consciously choosing to look closely at the buildings, appreciate the flowers, and savor the details, you reawaken that original sense of joy and appreciation. No external change is needed; only your perception must shift. This illustrates a fundamental truth: the difference between enjoying a moment and feeling indifferent to it lies in your awareness.

Awareness continuously shapes how we experience the world around us. Without it, even the most extraordinary environments or situations lose their charm. With it, even the simplest scenes can become sources of wonder and fulfillment. Ultimately, practicing awareness allows us to reclaim the richness of the present moment, transforming ordinary routines into extraordinary experiences.

8.1 Understanding Awareness

A powerful illustration of awareness comes from a social experiment involving the world-renowned violinist Joshua Bell. Picture a bustling subway station filled with the clamor of commuters and the echo of footsteps. Amidst this chaos, Bell, dressed as an ordinary street performer, begins to play his Stradivarius violin, worth 3.5 million dollars. His music, a mesmerizing symphony, fills the air. Just days earlier, Bell had performed to a sold-out audience where tickets averaged $100 each. Yet, in the subway, only six people stopped to listen during his 45-minute performance. The lack of awareness among the passersby made them miss a rare and beautiful moment. The chatter in our minds yells, 'No time for Mozart. We've got emails and existential dread to attend to!' All while a Stradivarius serenades us in the background. It's like ignoring a gourmet meal because you're too focused on reheating leftovers.

To be aware means we do not think of the future or the past and allow our senses to soak in everything external as well as internal. There is no judgment if what we experience is good or bad, we only experience. We do not compare the experience to the future or the past. It is the realization that there is no future and no past, just the eternal now. Any positive emotion can only arise in the now. Whenever we focus on a blissful experience in the future or the past, it will ultimately lead us to feel pain, as of right now, the situation is not as it will be or used to be. If we disregard the future and the past and focus on our awareness in the here and now, we create the space for positive emotions to arise. By training our mind in awareness, we increase our capacity for positive experiences.

A friend of mine, active on social media, once received a message accusing her of portraying an unrealistically perfect life. She was confused because she genuinely did not have many negative experiences. Her heightened awareness made her life appear exceptional. This wasn't due to luck but to her conscious effort in maintaining awareness. We cannot control happiness, but we can create conditions where it can flourish. But this also means we can create conditions where there is no space for happiness.

Quieting the mind is like hitting the mute button on that never-ending commentary track so you can finally hear the world's soundtrack. Instead of the internal monologue debating coffee vs. tea, you might hear the birds chirping, which is arguably more poetic. When not preoccupied with thoughts, we can fully engage our senses.

Now, we might have the misconception that the best way is to suppress thought. But this will only create internal resistance. In the worst case, we might even beat ourselves up for still thinking. One practice is to just observe our thoughts, and eventually, after observing them, they will quiet down. This practice is a huge part of meditation, and that is also one of the reasons why meditation increases the quality of your life. However, it is not the only way to practice it.

You can also consciously shift your awareness by focusing on the nice things again. It is especially easy when you remember how you walked along the beach, the mountains, or a flashy city when you were on holiday.

You were looking at your environment with fresh eyes. A feeling of novelty was coming up within you, and you were in awe of what nature or humans were able to create. You probably felt a feeling of gratitude for being there at this very moment to experience the amazing view while the wind was blowing through your hair. You felt alive in your body, feeling your heart pumping and your breath in your lungs.

Now summon up the same feeling while you are walking along the daily streets that you must walk on. Pretend you're a tourist in your city. Gawking at everyday sights like they're wonders of the world. Who knew that the coffee shop you pass daily could feel like a Parisian bistro with the right mindset? And hey, take selfies with landmarks no one else notices, like that oddly shaped tree or the graffiti that says, 'Jeff was here.' Take yourself some time and listen to music with full awareness. Allow yourself to see new things and feel your body. Be grateful for what you are seeing and inspire a feeling of awe within you.

Try either of these techniques for a while, and you will start to become a master of changing your state.

As awareness is bound to your senses, an easy way to increase your awareness is through physical activities. How can you not gain awareness of your body when learning a new skill like the handstand? Being able to command your body in the way that you want it to requires exceptional awareness. A painter needs to move his hands in a way that his mind is imagining the picture. As a yogi, you need to be able to relax your body in uncomfortable positions. There is no way to practice a physical skill without increasing our awareness. Thales answered the question „*What man is happy?*" with „*He who has a healthy body, a resourceful mind, and a docile nature.*"

Gratitude is a very effective way to cultivate awareness. If you are grateful for your experience, you are communicating to your mind that you are living in abundance. Gratitude whispers to your brain, 'Relax, you've got enough.' It's like being a squirrel who just hit the nut jackpot, feeling safe, sound, and thriving. When you feel thankful for what's around you, you give your brain a vacation from its usual 'doomsday prepper' mode. This will create space for happiness.

As we will find in a later chapter, it is the purpose of the mind to provide us with safety. It is hard-coded in our genes to associate resources as a form of safety. While there is objective safety, it is more important to feel safe regardless of the situation. In fact, we are probably living in the safest times ever. But most people will still feel insecure. The constant stream of negative news provides evidence within our minds of a dangerous world out there.

The feeling of safety, however, is built by finding evidence that nothing bad happens to us even though we are in new situations. So, instead of consuming the news, we can acquire evidence by stepping outside of our comfort zone. Stepping outside of your comfort zone does not mean that you need to do dangerous activities, like wingsuit flying. Just put yourself into new environments, like a market in a foreign country. This will create evidence that the world is safe. Slowly widening your comfort zone. If we do not take active measures to widen that comfort zone, then it will shrink.

Once we tell ourselves the story that we are safe and we can trust the world, it allows the mind to take a break. It might be short in the beginning, as the world is constantly requesting its capacities, but as we continue practicing it, the breaks will be longer. Eventually leading to inner peace.

We often confuse freedom with a genie granting us every wish. But the mind's wish list is endless. It's like trying to satisfy a toddler who just discovered candy. True freedom is ignoring the toddler's tantrum and appreciating the quiet beauty of a sunset instead. History is witness to this aspect of human nature, given the number of insatiable rulers we produced. True freedom arises when we are not entangled in what our ego is telling us. If you can do what you want and need to do despite your mind demanding something else, you truly are free. This freedom will create true abundance in your life. At that moment that realization happens, we will fully be aware within our body and our surroundings. A realization that there is a unity happening with our body and surroundings, a connection with the world.

The only thing you can control is your own behaviors and thoughts. This is what sets you apart from Machiavellian behavior. Among the dark triad of psychopaths, narcissists, and Machiavellians, the latter is the largest group, making up a staggering 16% of the population compared to 1% for narcissists. Despite this, they are the least discussed. Named after Niccolò Machiavelli, a philosopher who wrote 'The Prince' as a guide on ruling,

Machiavellians seek control without any moral consideration. The reason for mentioning them is to highlight how the desire for control can cause a lot of harm. We all want to control the world, especially when we think it's for the „*betterment*" of the world.

We usually desire what we don't have. At the heart of the desire for control lies a feeling of not having control. But isn't it ironic that even people with enormous power and influence still crave control? It seems counterintuitive, doesn't it? The world can never be completely controlled. It will always change, often in unexpected ways. When you try to force your will onto it, it tends to backfire. It doesn't matter how much you accumulate. In fact, the more you have, the more you stand to lose. Ancient kings felt so insecure that they had guards hidden in walls to guard their other guards. The misconception is seeking control outside us. You can never fully control the world, but you can control yourself. A person who has control over themselves doesn't need all the glory or riches in the world. This means that most Buddhas die silently.

8.2 The Impact of Awareness on Well-being

Awareness also helps us deal with guilt and unmet expectations. If guilt arises without harm, it's likely influenced by external sources and is unproductive. Spotting guilt early is like noticing a weird smell in the fridge. You deal with it before it turns into a full-blown disaster. Otherwise, it festers, attracting manipulative people like leftover pizza attracts ants. Letting go of expectations requires awareness, especially when reality doesn't align with them. Our minds often resist, but awareness allows us to let go and make rational decisions.

It seems especially hard to let go of things that we have already invested a large amount of time and resources. This is called the sunk cost fallacy. This is the main reason why we hold on to a path that does not suit us anymore. This might be something minor, as standing in line in the supermarket that is moving very slowly, unwilling to change to the line next to ours, since we already have waited so long at our current one. It can also be a big decision. Imagine you have already invested 30 years of your life into an ideology, a person, or an unsuccessful business. It will be very hard to admit to yourself that all this time was wasted.

Meet Paul, an inhabitant of Auroville. Which, for privacy reasons, is not his real name. If you want to live in Auroville, you must first work for one year for free, and if the community accepts you, then you must give up on your worldly possessions. Everything is owned by the community, and no one has their own possessions. It is a truly astonishing place for spiritual practices. They have a giant golden orb in the center of the community, with

121

different places to meditate or pray. While this might be a beautiful community for some, it can be a prison for others.

Paul was not happy in the place he decided to move to 30 years ago. All the spiritual practices did not seem to help elevate his depression. On the contrary, he arrived in the place happy and with high hopes. But throughout the years, he felt as if he was stuck. He could not say anything against the community either, as the house that he built during the 30 years of staying there was not his but owned by the community. If he were thrown out of the community, he would lose all his belongings from one moment to the next. All his social contacts would be lost in a heartbeat. Even if he wanted to leave, he had not even a penny to his name. He could not even buy a bus ticket to Delhi.

As an outsider, the answer seemed awfully simple. It seems so simple because we are not the person who has to let go of something. He would literally lose everything he knows if he left. Not knowing that on the other side awaits freedom. Oftentimes, we are stuck in similar situations, and we stay in a situation, place, or social group because we have already invested so much, and leaving it would mean we would lose it all. Not only is the ego fighting it, but it must let go of the outside world, creating this. We also fight it because that would mean the very things that defined us would have to die. It means survival or death for our ego. With our survival instinct kicking in, it becomes a very serious matter, doesn't it?

To my knowledge, Paul did not leave his community. But maybe we are stuck in the same way. The chances are that it might not even be evident to us.

Some might say it was unfortunate, but as life is the best teacher, it was a lucky lesson I learned early on. I invested many years in my religious community. It wasn't entirely wasted; there was an exchange of value. It gave me a sense of belonging, a higher purpose, and security in an uncertain world. Especially since I wasn't popular at school, and the uncertainties at home played their part too. However, admitting that my belief in God was irrational and not based on objective evidence was very painful. It meant being ostracized from the community where I spent most of my time and realizing that all my work for the community was wasted. All my efforts to appeal to God were futile as well. Naturally, these realizations hurt a lot. But it was a valuable lesson many never learned. People strongly identify with their communities and surroundings to the point where they can't imagine life without them. When making important choices, the sunk cost fallacy heavily influences decisions.

Take a job, for example. You studied for years and have expertise in a specific field. Letting go of this path seems devastating. We fear the unknown path. What if we can't make a living on the new path? It feels like an existential threat. People get stuck in their minds' prisons, unable to change their path. The sunk cost fallacy greatly influences our lives, but it's not the only logical fallacy that affects us.

Awareness permeates all aspects of life. It can be the difference between making a conscious decision in a heated moment and observing the trajectory of our chosen path. Ask yourself: Will the path you're on lead to the goals you want to achieve? You can't expect to become a renowned scientist without studying, but instead, party every weekend and waste your brain on drugs. Similarly, you can't become a famous DJ by staying in university and never going out. Are you doing things to avoid pain, or are they genuinely bringing you closer to who you want to become? Chances are you'll need to let go of your current path, habits, location, and maybe even the people around you. Yes, even if that means saying goodbye to your favorite Friday night pizza ritual with Debbie from HR.

You might feel reluctant because the pain is pulling you apart. Picture yourself in twenty years, stuck in the same rut. Do you really want 'Could Have Been' to be your memoir's title? Sure, change is scary, but so is realizing you've been rewatching the same boring episode of your life for decades. You'll become bitter because the world changed around you while you played it safe. Seeing someone else who left the same path you were on and improved their life will sting. It shows who you could have been. Your ego will rationalize why they succeeded and you didn't. Bitter people blame the world, but deep down, they know no one else is to blame. They are angry at themselves, but their ego doesn't allow that realization, so they blame the world, keeping them in constant pain.

If you rehearse your day in the evening, asking yourself, *„Did this action bring me closer to who I want to become or further away?"* you can do this while meditating or journaling. Remember to love yourself in the process. You are not a machine but a human with needs.

Awareness is important on all levels life has to offer. It can increase our experience of the moment, but it can also help us realize where we are standing right now and where we are heading. It is the difference between repeating a programmed pattern within our mind and just observing what's happening. We are all system-blind, but if we can see what is happening without judgment, a new path might open. One way to describe this is like shifting your perspective in a video game from being the character to being the player. As the player, you are seeing more of the entire picture, while the video game character would be very limited in his perception. While the player is going on an adventure with his character, the character would be confused about how so much misfortune could happen to him. You are not scared of the spiders attacking the character as the player, but the character would be in fear. But maybe it was needed to level up to deal with the spiders.

8.3 Wu Wei

In our pursuit of mastery, we often find ourselves entangled in relentless doing, convinced that the path to achievement lies solely in action. Yet, an essential truth illuminated by ancient wisdom is often overlooked: mastery also resides in non-action; this is what the Taoists call Wu Wei, or effortless action. This principle, known as Wu Wei, invites us to explore a way of acting that flows naturally with life's currents.

Wu Wei does not imply passivity or laziness. Rather, it signifies acting in harmony with the natural flow of life. Imagine water navigating through a riverbed: it exerts no force yet moves powerfully around obstacles, carving paths without struggle. Similarly, when we align ourselves with our inner truth and the natural rhythm of life, our actions arise spontaneously, free from resistance and stress.

This understanding leads us directly into a deeper exploration of the distinction between Being and Doing.

Doing is outward-focused and goal-oriented; it arises from a desire to control, achieve, or change something external. Doing often involves mental chatter, strategic planning, and a relentless pursuit of future outcomes, leaving little room for inner peace or genuine presence. It is driven primarily by the ego's desire to validate itself through measurable achievements and external validation.

Being, however, is inwardly oriented and inherently present. It is a state of profound awareness and deep alignment with the current moment. In Being, there's no frantic search for the next moment or next achievement.

It involves surrendering fully to the experience of now, accepting reality without judgment or resistance. This doesn't mean that action ceases; rather, actions naturally flow from a place of calm, clarity, and intuitive wisdom.

Consider a musician deeply absorbed in music, or an athlete immersed in their sport. They are not consumed by thoughts of performing actions; rather, they are the actions themselves. They embody the state of Being so completely that Doing becomes effortless, almost as if guided by an unseen force.

Cultivating Wu Wei in our daily lives begins with awareness. It involves observing without immediate reaction, recognizing the impulse to control or resist, and then consciously choosing to relax into acceptance. This subtle shift from Doing into Being opens space for intuition, creativity, and wisdom to arise naturally.

As you move forward in your journey of self-awareness, reflect on moments when effortlessness emerged naturally. What conditions enabled this flow? What resistance or fear dissolved in those moments? Embracing Wu Wei isn't about abandoning ambition; it's about allowing your ambitions to unfold from a state of inner harmony and genuine presence.

In mastering the art of Wu Wei, you begin to understand the transformative power of acting without forcing, of creating without striving, and ultimately, of living without unnecessary struggle.

8.4 Practical Techniques for Developing Awareness

Meditation is a powerful tool for cultivating awareness. There are many paths and forms of meditation, so find what works best for you. One approach is to start with a body scan and then observe thoughts without giving them any judgment. In the words of Dan Millman: „*You don't have to control your thoughts. You just have to stop letting them control you*". The goal is to transfer this awareness into daily life, becoming a „*living Buddha*" rather than just a „*sitting Buddha.*"

Here is a guide to a body scan meditation:

1. Find a comfortable sitting position
2. Close your eyes
3. Breathe in, feeling how it energizes your body
4. Breathe out, feeling how your body relaxes
5. Focus on the crown of your head and feel any sensations
6. Move your focus to the back of your head and feel any sensations
7. Move your focus to the forehead and feel any sensations
8. Move your focus to your eyes and how they feel in their sockets
9. Move your focus to your nose, stay here for a while, and observe your breath
10. Move your focus to your mouth and feel any tastes present
11. Move your focus to your throat and feel any sensations

12. Move your focus to your shoulders, feel if they are under tension or heavy
13. Move your focus to your arms, feel any sensation
14. Move your focus to your hands and all the sensations your hands can have
15. Move your focus to your heart and chest, feeling how your heart is beating and radiating energy into your body
16. Move your focus to the solar plexus and the sensations present
17. Move your focus to your sacrum, feel the ground below you, and your weight
18. Move your focus to your legs and the pressure from the ground
19. Move your focus to your feet and your toes
20. Sit in silence, listen to your inner chatter, or focus on things you want to manifest

Do everything at your own pace. The more conscious you are about every single sensation you can be, the better. If there is itching or other feelings of slight discomfort, you leave them be. You can change the direction from the feet to the crown if it suits you better. You can also do the body scan in both directions and repeatedly at a fast pace. Maybe it helps you imagine wind or water flowing through you. Experiment with it and do it however you like. Listen to other guided meditations as inspiration for finding your own way.

8.5 Illusion of Stillness

Meditation is often mistaken for silence. But true awareness is not about stillness alone. It is about presence. If it does not bring kindness into daily life, it is nothing more than a performance.

There was a man who meditated daily. As a Yoga teacher, he created an image of serenity, wisdom, and supposed mastery of the mind. But his son knew another version of him. At home, the man's stillness was fragile. His peace lasted only as long as no one disturbed him. One evening, as he sat in meditation, his son unknowingly interrupted him.

His father's eyes snapped open. His face twisted, breath sharp. „Can you not be quiet for once?" he hissed. The boy shrank back. He did not understand meditation, but he understood this: Whatever his father was seeking in those hours of silence, it had not made him a good father, because true peace comes from feeling connected to all things, not shutting them out.

True awareness is not found in stillness alone. It is revealed in how we respond when the world does not obey our wishes. If meditation does not extend beyond the cushion, it is hollow. To be only a sitting Buddha and not a living Buddha is to miss the very essence of the practice.

9 Letting Go
Finding Peace in Change

Let's introduce a concept that may feel unsettling at first but ultimately offers profound liberation: letting go. While initially uncomfortable, this skill becomes the bedrock upon which many other abilities rest. Courage, adaptability, resilience, and emotional balance are just a few examples. Indeed, being able to let go not only frees your mind but also makes life more fluid and enjoyable. By releasing what no longer serves us, we make space for growth, fresh perspectives, and maybe even a little room to finally remember where you left your peace of mind. Probably under that pile of unnecessary worries.

Consider how much of our suffering stems from holding onto things, be it ideas, expectations, possessions, or relationships, that were once helpful but have now become obstacles. Letting go provides a premise for change; it allows us to move forward, evolve, and discover more authentic ways of being. In previous discussions, we explored how observing our thoughts and emotions enables us to navigate life with greater awareness. Letting go is the next step, transforming that insight into action. To fully embrace this liberation, we must explore how letting go reshapes our relationship with ourselves and the world.

As we delve deeper, we'll examine the essence of non-attachment, see how releasing resistance enhances discipline and contentment, and understand why shedding outdated identities or beliefs is often necessary to uncover our true selves. Letting go is not about giving up on life; rather, it's about freeing ourselves from unnecessary burdens so that life's natural flow can guide us toward richer experiences, inner peace, and a more genuine sense of self.

9.1 The Fundamentals of Non-Attachment

The concept of letting go has deep roots in wisdom traditions. Siddhartha Gautama, the first Buddha, framed it as „*non-attachment*"—a state of being unbound by possessions, expectations, or fixed ideas. To be non-attached doesn't mean you don't care; rather, it means you are willing to release what no longer serves you, whether it's an object you once cherished, a relationship, or a rigid belief about the world. Therefore, we embrace the fluidity of an ever-changing reality, accepting it as it unfolds. By reframing „non-attachment" as *„letting go,"* we highlight the inner intensity of this shift. We're not just refusing to cling to something; we're actively releasing emotional knots that keep our minds from flowing freely.

This mental flexibility is crucial because it allows us to adapt gracefully when life changes course. The more we practice letting go, the more we find ourselves navigating around obstacles with ease, much like water finding its path around stones in a stream. Bruce Lee, though often quoted to the point of cliché, captured this perfectly: „Empty your mind, be formless, shapeless—like water. Now, you put water in a cup, it becomes the cup; you put water into a bottle, it becomes the bottle; you put it in a teapot, it becomes the teapot. Now water can flow, or it can crash. Be water, my friend."

While such imagery may be familiar, its truth endures. When we cease to cling tightly to what we think we must have or be, we begin to *flow* more naturally around life's curves. By cultivating non-attachment, we free ourselves from unnecessary constraints, thus laying a foundation for the inner harmony and adaptability that make genuine transformation possible. Think of non-attachment as unsubscribing from those spam emails your ego keeps sending: „URGENT: You NEED this to be happy!" Spoiler alert—you don't.

9.2 Letting Go in Everyday Life

When we first consider letting go, we often think of material possessions. Losing a wallet or crashing a car can feel devastating, yet after the initial shock, no amount of emotional turmoil will restore what was lost. We might brood for days, caught in a loop of regret or anger, until, at last, we accept reality and release our attachment. At that moment, life becomes easier again. This pattern appears frequently in our lives: the suffering ends not because something external changed, but because we let go of our internal struggle. The ability to set things free, whether objects, situations, or outcomes, is a crucial skill that underlies many others.

This principle also applies to more subtle circumstances, such as the mismatch between our internal expectations and the world as it is. Acceptance is needed only when our beliefs, values, or desires fail to align with reality. We have a choice: continue resisting what we cannot change, prolong our suffering, or let go of the mental constructs causing this tension. Whether we are grappling with the profound loss of a loved one or facing a minor inconvenience like taking out the garbage, letting go creates space for acceptance. Only by relinquishing our grip on how things „*should*"be can we find peace in how they actually are.

The same logic transforms our understanding of discipline. Contrary to popular belief, true discipline isn't about mustering willpower to bulldoze through unwanted tasks. That approach, while possible in the short term, drains energy and motivation. Instead, discipline arises naturally when we let go of inner resistance. Consider the desire to learn guitar. If you don't practice, it's not that you lack motivation; it's that you're holding onto some form of internal resistance, maybe a feeling that this obligation limits your freedom. By releasing that resistance and acting immediately when it surfaces, you create a momentum that builds discipline effortlessly. Each time you let go of hesitation and follow through, you reinforce a habit without fighting yourself. Over time, this saves considerable energy and prevents the exhaustion of constantly „*pushing through*" life's tasks.

Letting go also opens the door to genuine contentment. Although we live with unprecedented access to material wealth, many still struggle to feel satisfied. Instead of appreciating what we have, we fixate on what we lack or what others display on social media. This fuels envy and greed rather than gratitude. By letting go of these insatiable desires, we discover that contentment doesn't stem from accumulation; it comes from recognizing our present abundance. As Socrates observed, „*Contentment is natural wealth; luxury is artificial poverty.*" Freeing ourselves from the illusion that we always need more allows us to become naturally rich in spirit.

A similar principle applies to personal growth. Sometimes, what holds us back from being better communicators, more empathetic listeners, or more confident individuals is our own inner narrative. Stories we tell ourselves about why we cannot change. Our ego excels at generating excuses and reinforcing old identities, beliefs, and habits. These patterns, often learned early in life and reinforced through biases like anchoring or confirmation bias, keep us tethered to stale versions of ourselves. To chart a new path, we must let go of these outdated self-concepts. In doing so, we open ourselves to new possibilities, making genuine transformation possible.

This brings us to a common paradox in self-improvement and spirituality: we're urged both to „grow" and to accept that we are already enough. On the surface, it sounds contradictory. If we are enough, why must we change? But the key lies in understanding that true growth comes from shedding what isn't real or helpful, not from piling on more layers. Improving communication skills or becoming more diligent might enhance our daily lives, but our deepest spiritual evolution comes from letting go of harmful habits, distorted perceptions, and false identities. Visualize it like peeling an onion: each layer removed brings us closer to the core essence of who we truly are. In German, the word *entwickeln*, often translated as „to develop" or „to grow," literally means „to untangle" or „to unfold." This offers a more precise image of growth, not as accumulation, but as a process of unraveling the knots that keep us bound, revealing what has been present all along. As Alan Watts famously noted, trying to define our true self is as futile as „biting our own teeth."

It is something to experience and not to be described. It's not about achieving some grand new self; it's about releasing the clutter that obscures our innate wholeness.

Realizing this dissolves the supposed paradox. We are inherently enough, but to „grow," we must continuously let go of limiting beliefs, unnecessary judgments, and the armor we think protects us. Without seeing ourselves as fundamentally sufficient, we'll mistake these layers of fear and resistance for essential parts of our being. Letting them go gradually thins the membrane between us and the world, making life easier, lighter, and more authentic. Operating from a state of lack only feeds the ego's delusions, whereas recognizing our intrinsic completeness frees us from internal resistance and the suffering it generates.

In everyday life, letting go means dropping the struggle against reality, against ourselves, and against the flow of time and change. By mastering this art, we not only reduce unnecessary suffering but also create the mental and emotional space needed to thrive, adapt, and fully engage with life's unfolding opportunities.

9.3 Transforming Suffering by Letting Go

As I mentioned before, my father's death was one of the most profound learning experiences of my life. The pain of facing a future without him felt overwhelming. Many people believe their grief is for the one who passed, but in truth, the departed feel no pain. No matter if you envision them in heaven, reincarnated, at peace in nirvana, or simply gone. The grief we experience is for ourselves.

Before we explore how to transform suffering by letting go, allow me to address the broader context of our societal relationship with death. In modern times, death is almost a taboo subject. We keep it at arm's length, hiding it away in hospitals or funeral homes. Historically, however, death was more openly woven into daily life. Our avoidance does a disservice to our consciousness, hindering our ability to accept that our time here is limited. By refusing to acknowledge our mortality, we miss the opportunity to find peace and purpose. In fact, understanding and embracing mortality can be a powerful motivator to live fully.

When we truly accept that death can come at any moment, holding onto painful emotions or grievances becomes senseless. If life is brief and unpredictable, why waste even a moment clinging to feelings that only multiply our suffering? The thought of our mortality isn't meant to frighten us; rather, it's a gentle reminder urging us to release whatever steals our peace, freeing us to savor each experience deeply and authentically.

I have come to terms with mortality three times. The first time was through my childhood Christian faith. In that belief system, death leads to heaven. A form of ultimate salvation rather than punishment, assuming you discard the notion of hell. Ironically, many Christians seem unsure about this promise, as there's no grand celebration when someone dies, even though it should herald their arrival in paradise.

Later, as I shifted towards atheism, I needed to reconcile with death once more. Without religious assurances, death can feel like a frightening void. We often mistake death for a kind of lonely imprisonment in darkness. But that fear is more about loneliness than death itself. Without consciousness, there is no experience, neither good nor bad. It's akin to the state before you were born: nothingness. When facing mortality directly, people often share regrets rooted in not having truly lived. In that moment, material possessions and ambitions seem inconsequential.

My third encounter with mortality came during a psychedelic experience. Although I promised not to delve too deeply into mystical realms for now, I believe sharing a bit of this perspective may be illuminating. In this altered state, everything that defines your unique self, including your scars, suffering, and pain, dissolves. It offers a glimpse of what one might call heaven or an existence where you share consciousness with all that is, merging into a unified whole. There's a sublime, geometric beauty to this experience that can move anyone to tears, not just math enthusiasts like me. It's timeless and infinite, where past and future incarnations exist simultaneously.

This perspective temporarily aligns the subconscious and conscious mind, releasing attachments such as toxic relationships and fears. If we are all the same consciousness playing a grand game with ourselves, then all suffering is self-inflicted. This insight answers Epicurus's paradox more elegantly than „God works in mysterious ways." From that vantage point, it's as though I have already died once. Why fear dying again if each death merely signals the end of a temporary manifestation of consciousness, allowing a new adventurer to take its place?

Returning to my father's death, I found myself struggling with an internal conflict between how I believed the world should be and how it actually was. This inner friction caused me to spiral negatively. At that time, I lived in a student dorm with people I had not chosen as my roommates. One individual claimed to have depression, and while I initially felt compassion and excused his inability to perform basic tasks like cleaning, I unknowingly contributed to a toxic dynamic. As Stephen Karpman's drama model explains, enabling someone's excuses is a disservice to both parties. Because I lacked practice in letting go and was still coping with my father's death, my irritation grew. I expected fair treatment, but when he damaged my belongings, I received only toxic responses: stealing, tantrums, slammed doors, lies, manipulation, and even threatening displays like butterfly knives on the kitchen table.

Any toxic relationship requires at least two participants. My roommate and I both held expectations about how the world should be, which clashed with the reality we faced. Ironically, we shared the same root cause of suffering: the discord between our inner expectations and the external world. Had I been more emotionally aware, I could have recognized my frustration and responded more responsibly. Instead, I let annoyance grow into resentment, bitterness, anger, and, finally, suffering.

Negative emotions rarely travel solo. They bring their whole crew: self-doubt, desire for control, unnecessary drama, and that one friend who loves to point out your flaws at family gatherings. Yet, this experience was valuable. If I had been more flexible with my expectations or learned to let go sooner, things might have turned out differently. We often see different „sides" of people depending on how we act towards them. Responsibility rests in our ability to respond differently, easing our path through life rather than trying to change its unyielding tides.

When suffering becomes unbearable, we reach a breaking point. We can either remain broken or rebuild ourselves. This is the difference between growing from trauma and using it as a crutch. Our ego fiercely clings to old narratives, turning us into „broken records" if we let it. But there is a different approach. The Japanese art of Kintsugi involves repairing broken pottery with gold or silver lacquer, making the once-fractured piece more beautiful and valuable than before. It teaches us that scars are not shameful; they are testaments to resilience and growth. Similarly, letting go of old stories and expectations can transform suffering into wisdom and compassion, leaving us more whole and radiant.

To repair myself, I had to forgive myself. Clinging to truth and fairness wasn't worth the suffering it caused. Paradoxically, accepting this helped me process my father's death. I had to let go on multiple levels: letting go of my father's presence, my rigid sense of justice, and material attachments. Feeling the pain instead of wrestling with it brought a surprising sense of relief, kind of like realizing you've been pushing a door marked 'pull' the whole time. Acceptance ended my suffering and revealed a straightforward solution: moving out of the dorm. With acceptance, I could stop taking my roommate's tantrums personally and appreciate having had a loving father rather than resenting the world. After all, suffering does not occur outside of us; it is how we respond to what happens. Suffering emerges when we judge pain instead of experiencing it as it is. Change the inner workings, and you remove suffering. This may sound extraordinary, but monks illustrate this principle through extraordinary feats of endurance. Some even remain unmoving while being burned alive. An unimaginable act to a suffering mind, yet they accomplish it by accepting pain rather than suppressing it.

We need not become monks to understand this principle. Practicing with any form of discomfort can teach us. Take ice bathing, for example: if you enter the icy water and immediately focus on the pain, you tense up, suffer intensely, and count every agonizing second. Alternatively, if you step into the cold, notice the sensations, breathe steadily, and relax each muscle as tension arises, you accept the discomfort instead of fighting it. This shift in mindset allows you to remain in the ice bath much longer. Physically, the pain signals are the same, but by accepting them, acknowledging them, and letting them pass, you remain resilient. You can apply this approach to other situations of discomfort, be it exercise, dealing with screaming babies on airplanes, or any challenging experience.

The process of letting go is simple yet difficult. It varies by situation, but certain steps remain consistent. First, identify what's causing your irritation. This alone can sometimes dissolve the fear. If you realize you possess the skills or resources to overcome a challenge, your fear may vanish. In more complex situations, name the emotion itself. Feel it fully without judgment. Judging your emotions creates resistance and prevents them from flowing naturally. Become aware of both the emotion and any resistance it stirs. Just observing allows them to dissolve. With practice, this awareness without judgment becomes your gateway to letting go.

Often, our suffering lingers not because of the emotions themselves, but due to our avoidance or resistance to feeling them fully. Imagine confronting a scary clown. Initially, it's intimidating, and you may feel the urge to run away. But what happens if you simply sit down with the clown, maybe even engage it in conversation? Soon enough, it loses its power over you; the fear dissolves, and what was once frightening becomes harmless, perhaps even comical. The same holds true for other difficult emotions. Allow yourself to sit quietly with feelings such as fear, grief, or anger. By acknowledging their presence without judgment or resistance, you will find that their intensity naturally diminishes. In this way, emotions lose their grip, revealing themselves as temporary visitors rather than permanent threats.

When my father died, I suffered because my inner image of reality did not match the actual world. Each time I faced the pain, I resisted it, pushing it away. Positive emotions we allow to dance within us freely, knowing we cannot control their duration, so we simply enjoy them. Negative emotions, however, we resist. In doing so, we never let them finish their dance. They remain unresolved and reemerge in uglier forms, such as anger, depression, or self-pity, continually denying reality. To end this cycle, we must practice forgiveness, removing the judgment that fuels resistance. Forgiveness does not mean forgetting; it means releasing the emotional charge that binds you to the past.

A common misconception is that you must re-experience your trauma fully to heal. This is unnecessary and can be counterproductive. You only need to feel your emotions fully and without judgment. Otherwise, you risk deepening the wound rather than healing it.

When letting go is difficult, follow this process:

1. **Identify the Core Emotion:**
   Begin by recognizing the true emotion beneath the surface. For example, anger or hatred may mask deeper feelings like fear, insecurity, or grief. Becoming aware of what's truly arising helps direct your attention to the root cause rather than its symptoms.

2. **Examine Your Expectations:**
   Notice where your internal picture of how things „should" be conflicts with reality. This clash often fuels resistance and discomfort. Understanding the discrepancy can sometimes dissolve fear on its own simply by revealing that you have the resources, skills, or safety nets you need.

3. **Observe Without Judgment:**
   Allow the emotion to be present without labeling it as „good" or „bad." Imagine the emotion as a dancer on the stage of your awareness. Instead of pushing it off the stage, let the dancer complete its routine. When you refrain from resisting, suppressing, or clinging, the emotion can finish its natural course and subside more easily.

4. **Practice Forgiveness and Acceptance:**
   If the emotion persists or feels overwhelming, practice forgiveness toward yourself and others to release any lingering emotional charge. Acceptance doesn't mean endorsing harmful

behavior or ignoring injustice. It means acknowledging the reality of a situation so you can respond, rather than react, from a place of clarity and calm.

5. **Stay Present and Relax the Body:**
   When the mind inevitably wanders or tries to replay old stories, guide it gently back to the present moment. Focus on your breath, your bodily sensations, or the immediate environment. With each breath, notice tension dissolving in your muscles. As the emotion completes its „*dance*," you'll feel the subtle shift as suffering eases and clarity returns.

6. **Align Inner and Outer Reality:**
   Once the emotion settles, you'll find that your inner world aligns more closely with the outer world. From this state of balance, you can make choices, either practical actions in the physical world or mindful adjustments in your thinking, without creating new resistance. This is where authentic change and healing unfold.

With the emotional burden lifted, you can take constructive steps, physical changes in your environment or subtle shifts in thought, without generating new resistance. Like a Tai Chi master, move smoothly through life's currents, applying force only when necessary.

If suffering returns, that's okay. We are all human. The ego, which conceals the true origin of our emotions and creates resistance, is persistent. By practicing awareness and letting go, we learn to navigate pain, transform suffering into understanding, and find beauty, even in our brokenness.

10 Responsibility
Taking Command of Your Journey

We all have responsibilities. What a dreadful word, isn't it? Responsibility often carries a negative connotation in our society. It's seen as a burden, an obligation, or a constraint that limits our freedom and spontaneity. Yet, responsibilities are unavoidable. On the contrary, if we do not respond to them, the consequences will create even more challenges than they originally brought. It is important to note that responsibilities will cause pain regardless of whether you do the task or avoid it. The only difference is when you will face the pain and whether it occurs on your terms. It is the difference between getting caught in the rain and taking a shower. If we take the shower, we internally consent to the experience, while we are less likely to consent when caught off guard. Even the experience of walking through the rain can be enjoyable if we accept it.

Another misconception about responsibility is that we should take on all the world's burdens or accept blame. You're not Atlas, and the world doesn't need you to hold it up. After all, „*responsibility*" stems from the word „*response.*" Instead of reacting to the world, we need to respond to it. A person who responds is responsible, while one who reacts is irresponsible. A reaction is an unconscious event to the environment, while a response requires awareness of what is happening before we make a conscious decision. If it is a conscious decision, it means you should do it wisely. It is the difference between acting on our emotions and thoughts impulsively and observing them without judgment before we act.

10.1 Responding Instead of Reacting

Here, the concept of the locus of control comes into play. Your locus of control refers to the extent to which you believe you have control over the events in your life. Those with an internal locus of control believe they can influence their circumstances through their actions, whereas those with an external locus of control feel their lives are dictated by external forces. Responsibility and an internal locus of control are intrinsically linked. When you view yourself as the captain of your ship, you acknowledge that you have the power to steer it, even amidst turbulent seas. This perspective allows you to respond, rather than react, to challenges.

Let's assume you have teenage children and one of them destroys a very precious item. Besides being expensive, it might hold emotional value to you. In a fit of rage, you might say something that damages your relationship with your child. The things you say might be so hurtful that they threaten their survival mechanism. Maybe you will remedy the situation with a lot of effort, but maybe this will be a permanently scarring experience for your child. In the best-case scenario, you will become the subject of a TikTok titled „*My Parent Went Full Karen.*"

A responsible approach would be to take a moment to calm down before addressing the situation. Gather the facts instead of making accusations. Ask calmly if everything is okay and what happened. By asking questions first in a calm tone, you're modeling the responsible behavior of open communication that you want to see in your child. Listen to their explanation without interrupting or judging. Now, you've created the space to have a conversation about their actions. A responsible approach shows you're conscious of your emotions, open to discussion, and focused on guiding them toward proper behavior, not just lashing out in anger over one mistake. This models the level-headedness you want to instill.

The way you respond in this scenario reflects your locus of control. An external locus of control might lead you to blame your child entirely, feeling like a victim of their actions. In contrast, an internal locus of control helps you recognize that your response can shape the outcome and the future of your relationship.

I think back to our family's strawberry farm, where responsibility wasn't just a concept; it was something we had to face head-on every winter night. Frost was our biggest adversary, capable of destroying entire fields of strawberries in a single freezing night. The solution wasn't glamourous: someone had to get up in the middle of the night to turn on the sprinklers. When the water froze, it formed a protective layer of ice that insulated the plants from the harsh cold.

In the beginning, it was my father who shouldered this task. Night after night, he would wake up, bundle himself in layers, and head out into the freezing dark to protect the fields. It wasn't easy, but he didn't complain. He understood that the survival of the farm, and by extension our family, depended on him. Over time, the responsibility shifted to my brother, who took on the task with the same quiet determination.

Looking back, I can see how this midnight ritual taught us the power of an internal locus of control. The frost was beyond our control. We couldn't stop it, argue with it, or wish it away. But we could choose how to respond. My father, and later my brother, didn't waste time resenting the cold or blaming external circumstances. Instead, they focused on the one thing they could control: turning on the sprinklers to protect what mattered most. This proactive mindset ensured the crops survived and the farm thrived.

Watching them taught me that responsibility isn't just about solving problems. It's about owning your role in the outcome. It's the difference between feeling like a victim of the frost and realizing you have the power to mitigate its effects. My father and brother didn't wait for perfect conditions; they acted with foresight and commitment, turning those freezing nights into moments of quiet triumph.

10.2 Responsibility as a Path to Freedom

We all desire a healthy body, but do you love your body? If you loved your body, wouldn't it mean you take great care of it? Working out regularly, giving it proper nourishment, and allowing it to regenerate? The responsible path to a healthy body involves a certain amount of discomfort. If, however, you decide to indulge in the comfort of the couch and unhealthy foods, you will have to bear the consequences later anyway.

There is a bittersweet realization here: The expression of love is correlated with taking responsibility. Love reciprocates. Your body will return the favor of being treated responsibly. The same is true for children or pets; they will return the best thing they have to offer, which is their unconditional love, except maybe cats because they have their own rules. Love in a romantic relationship is no different. Your willingness to sacrifice some of your time and well-being shows your love for the other person.

Love is the moment when your ego has no bearing on your interaction with the world. Such an action, without any ulterior motive, is a selfless act. It displays a healthy relationship with the ego, as it means you are not in constant survival mode. People who are stressed display more selfish behavior, as proven by every hangry person ever. Describing love in such pragmatic terms might seem unromantic, but it highlights a trait essential for parenthood. Two people acting selflessly guarantee the best survival for their offspring. They display the required responsibility to be parents.

But let me ask the question romantically: What would it mean to expand your responsibility and unconditional love to your entire world? The unconditional is an important keyword here. You do not love the world under a certain condition. You don't demand it to change in your image. This means that amidst all the chaos, one more peaceful island will be born. The only person you truly can change is yourself, after all, no? Only when you are at peace with yourself can you guide others toward their peace. What a conundrum it is for those who force their peace. This journey toward peace begins with taking responsibility for our own well-being, rooted in love for ourselves.

If you love yourself, this also means that you will take responsibility for your own life. The instant you expect others to take responsibility for aspects of your life, you give away the little power you have within your own life. Loving the world indicates that the world owes you nothing. Lifting this burden frees you. The world acts like a mirror reflecting any intent you put out. If you put out love, it will reciprocate.

Only if you take responsibility can you become truly free. If you think someone else should provide for your safety, wealth, or happiness, then that means you are not in control. It means someone else decides how much you should gain. The captain of a ship shoulders all the responsibility, and, therefore, he is the one in command. Even if the crew demands more freedom, without taking responsibility, they can't steer the boat. Once you demonstrate that you can take on responsibility, the world will take notice and provide you with more freedom and new opportunities. It means you can do the challenging tasks and learn to enjoy the challenge. It also means that your attention is not diverted by things that do not matter. If responsibilities feel overwhelming, remember that everyone who has taken command of their life has felt this way. Instead of pushing responsibility away, we need to change our perspective.

Realizing that taking responsibility generates abundance, purpose, and freedom in our lives can create a profound shift in perspective. We only perceive responsibilities as burdens if we judge ourselves harshly. When we constantly evaluate ourselves against unrealistic expectations, responsibilities can become overwhelming. The weight feels too heavy, and we might retreat into comforting excuses instead of reclaiming our freedom, sabotaging ourselves in the process. However, if we accept our shortcomings and understand that we are at the beginning of a journey, the burden becomes lighter. This acceptance requires letting go of our preconceived image of ourselves.

There are no games that do not have challenges for the player to overcome; it makes a game interesting to play. Seeing responsibilities as challenges that make life a game worth playing might be an interesting shift of perspective. Embracing challenges that enrich our lives can dramatically enhance our experience. Perhaps you want to start your own business, have children, or write a book. These endeavors provide purpose and meaning, even if the results are not immediately tangible. They transform our self-perception and how others perceive us, showcasing characteristics of someone shaping their world rather than being shaped by it. By adhering to our responsibilities, we create undeniable evidence of this transformation. As our mind gathers enough evidence for a new reality, it shifts into that new reality. Self-worth is not inherent; it is built by consistently honoring our commitments. As mentioned earlier, making truthfulness a habit is crucial. For a non-delusional person, the only way to build self-worth is through integrity.

There's no need to rush. You can take on responsibilities at your own pace, according to your circumstances. Mental or physical limitations may add challenges, but it would be selfish for anyone to claim you cannot achieve your own freedom because of them. Draw inspiration from individuals like Stephen Hawking or Peter Overton, who have surmounted significant obstacles.

A prevalent mindset worth addressing is the belief that you must fight for your place in the sun. While this approach might be viable, it is also exhausting. Viewing life as a constant struggle to win can lead to burnout. It is all about winning this and that. But if you lose, it is devastating, and winning is a rather short-lived experience. It would be wiser to see the challenges life throws at us as games or in the context of a story in a movie. Feeling as if you must fight the challenges will not only build inner resistance but also create friction with the world. By following the principles in this book, you will find a feeling of peace and realize there is no need to fight for your spot in the sun. Instead of battling others, let them be themselves. The same applies to your inner self; you don't need to fight to get the things you want but rather let inner resistance arise, let it go, and then act. The inner peace you will gain from this will be invaluable.

11 Optimism
A Way to Navigate Through Life

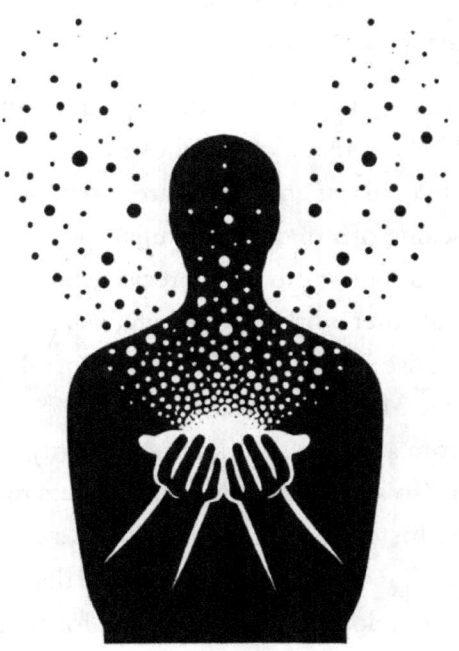

We often think happiness comes after success, as though it's a prize we earn only once we've achieved every goal. We tell ourselves, 'I'll be happy when I get the promotion,' or 'I'll finally relax after I hit my targets, ' like happiness is a mysterious, limited-edition reward available only after surviving capitalism's extreme obstacle course. The problem is that the finish line keeps moving; success continually shifts the goalpost, leaving happiness just out of reach. However, recent research in positive psychology challenges this notion and suggests we have the order reversed. In his book *The Happiness Advantage*, Shawn Achor explains that happiness isn't the result of success;

it's the cause. When we prioritize happiness first, we become more creative, productive, and resilient. In other words, a happy brain operates like high-speed internet, enabling us to load success efficiently, as opposed to the sluggish „*dial-up*" mindset we bring to tasks when we're stressed, anxious, or dissatisfied.

Despite mounting scientific evidence, some stubborn leaders still believe that a cheerful workforce is somehow less productive, that if employees are too happy, they must be slacking off. In contrast, universities now teach positive psychology to students precisely because future graduates will enter workplaces where, ironically, a simple smile might raise eyebrows. Yet here's the reality: happier employees are 31% more productive and 37% better at sales! Far from a liability, workplace positivity is like adding espresso shots to productivity. It gets things done with a smile. Instead of interpreting joy as a red flag, forward-thinking organizations recognize that content and engaged employees aren't just good for morale; they directly impact the bottom line. Yet, the power of optimism extends far beyond the office, shaping every corner of our lives.

Positive thinking shapes every domain of our lives, from personal relationships and health to career aspirations and community involvement. Approaching challenges with optimism allows you to spot opportunities where others see only obstacles. In relationships, focusing on what's good in others fosters trust, understanding, and warmth while mitigating the petty conflicts that can erode closeness. When working toward personal goals, optimism helps you remain motivated during setbacks, maintaining faith that progress, even if incremental, is possible. Even in life's toughest moments, choosing to find lessons and growth opportunities within adversity makes problems feel more manageable. Outside of professional spheres, embracing positivity isn't just about achieving success; it's about living more fully, creating stronger bonds, and facing life's twists and turns with confidence and resilience.

11.1 Practical Tools for Positivity

Cultivating optimism doesn't require dramatic, life-altering changes. Often, it's about small, intentional shifts in perspective, tiny recalibrations that slowly retrain your mind to focus on what's right rather than what's wrong. One of the simplest ways to begin this transformation is by embracing a practice that highlights life's blessings.

Practice Gratitude:

One of the most effective ways to start is by practicing gratitude. Spend a few moments each day reflecting on what you're thankful for, whether it's a supportive friend, a sunny morning, a meaningful conversation, or simply the fact that you have a moment to breathe and reset. This simple habit gently rewires your brain to notice life's positives, even amid challenges. Over time, the mind becomes more adept at scanning the environment for uplifting cues instead of defaulting to negativity.

Gratitude is deeply embedded in many cultures, each offering valuable lessons on how to incorporate appreciation into daily life. In Thai culture, for example, the concept of *Sanuk* emphasizes finding joy and worthiness in even the smallest moments, like savoring a shared meal, laughing with a friend, or greeting someone with a genuine smile. This mindset creates a ripple effect of positivity and connection. Immersing yourself in cultures or traditions that prioritize gratitude expands your perspective and normalizes optimism. It becomes less a chore and more a natural, life-giving habit.

Reframing Negative Thoughts:
Another powerful tool is reframing negative thoughts. When something goes wrong, challenge yourself to find another angle. A setback isn't necessarily a failure; it might be a redirection toward something better. By consciously choosing to see obstacles as opportunities for growth, you train your mind to approach problems with curiosity rather than defeat. This cognitive flexibility improves not just your mood but also your ability to adapt, learn, and evolve.

Environmental and Social Influences:
The people and places that surround you influence your mindset, often more than you realize. Spending time with individuals who uplift, support, and encourage you can reinforce your optimism. Similarly, even small adjustments to your environment, such as adding more natural light, including fresh plants, or incorporating vibrant colors, can improve your mood. Positive surroundings create a feedback loop that makes it easier to maintain an optimistic outlook.

The Power of a No-Complaints Challenge:
A practical, hands-on experiment is to challenge yourself to stop complaining for a month. Complaining, even casually, trains the mind to focus on what's wrong. By

consciously abstaining from airing gripes, you're forced to reframe situations and search for solutions or silver linings. For instance, if you're stuck in a long coffee shop line, resist the urge to gripe and instead listen to a podcast, plan your day, or appreciate the moment of pause. This isn't about suppressing genuine concerns. It's about breaking the habit of negativity and shifting your focus to more constructive or neutral thoughts. Over time, you'll find it easier to stay positive and embrace optimism as your default setting.

„Stop!": A Mental Reset Button:

When negativity spirals out of control, and your mind refuses to quiet down, try firmly saying „Stop!" in your head or even out loud if you're alone. Think of it as hitting the pause button on a dark, unsettling movie scene. This interrupting command disrupts the loop, giving you a moment to regain control and shift your thoughts toward something more balanced or productive. While this technique is most helpful when you're overwhelmed by racing thoughts, you'll find that as you grow more self-aware and skilled in other mindfulness practices, the need for this abrupt intervention may decrease. Still, it's a useful tool to have on hand when negative patterns threaten to dominate your mindset.

Focus on Solutions, Not Problems:

Embracing optimism also means directing energy toward solutions. Rather than dwelling on what's wrong, ask, „What can I do to improve this situation, even just a little?" Small, actionable steps restore a sense of control and keep you moving forward. Pair this solution-oriented approach with self-care techniques, such as a brisk walk, moments of deep breathing, or a brief stretching routine, to support both your body and mind. The synergy between physical well-being and mental outlook makes maintaining a positive perspective more effortless.

Celebrate the Wins—Big or Small:
Finally, remember to celebrate every bit of progress. Did you survive a tricky meeting? Nail a new recipe? Or, finally, fold that mountain of laundry? Pop the imaginary champagne, you've earned it. Remember, small wins count, too. For example, finding a matching pair of socks on laundry day. Recognizing these small victories reinforces the notion that you're growing, adapting, and thriving. Optimism isn't about pretending difficulties don't exist; it's about building the mindset and habits that let you face life's challenges with hope, perseverance, and confidence.

11.2 Cheerful positivity vs toxic positivity

In one of my many philosophical dives into the human condition with Rae, a friend of mine specializing in performance coaching, we stumbled upon the difference between toxic positivity and cheerful positivity. Cheerful positivity is rooted in authenticity. It comes from an excitement for life and is about finding joy and hope even during life's challenges while still acknowledging that difficulties exist. It allows room for genuine emotion, whether it's sadness, frustration, or grief, and allows optimism to move forward rather than dismiss the struggle. For instance, a friend practicing cheerful positivity might say, „*I know this is tough, but I'm here for you, and I believe you'll find a way through this."* It's uplifting without invalidating.

Toxic positivity is like slapping a 'Keep Smiling!' sticker on a sinking ship. It might look hopeful, but it's not exactly helpful. True positivity says, 'Hey, the ship's taking on water, but let's grab some buckets and bail together.' Toxic positivity is like putting on a mask, covering any genuine feelings for the sake of positivity. While the intention might be good, toxic positivity often silences important emotions and pressures people to hide their struggles, creating an unrealistic and unhealthy expectation to be happy all the time. This can leave individuals feeling isolated, unheard, or even ashamed of their feelings, as if experiencing pain or difficulty makes them somehow „*weak.*"

Cultivating genuine optimism doesn't mean masking or dismissing emotion. Instead, it involves acknowledging feelings for what they are, understanding their origins, and then choosing to move forward with greater wisdom. Imagine sitting across from a scary-looking clown. Your first reaction might be fear, and that fear is valid. Instead of running away or forcing yourself to feel „*happy,*" you simply acknowledge the fear: „*I'm scared right now.*" After giving yourself space to process that emotion, you try something different. Maybe you talk to the clown, ask about the story behind the costume, or find humor in the situation. By interacting authentically rather than avoiding the emotional truth, you transform your experience. What once was frightening becomes an opportunity for insight, human connection, and even laughter.

Ultimately, the goal of all these techniques, like gratitude, reframing thoughts, mindful interventions, and celebrating wins, is not to eradicate negative feelings but to put them in proper perspective. Emotions are like weather forecasts. They give you important info, but they don't control whether you pack an umbrella or sunglasses. With optimism, you become the meteorologist of your own emotional climate: *'Cloudy with a chance of gratitude.'* This balanced approach fosters growth, strengthens relationships, and allows you to face life's inevitable challenges with courage and compassion.

Cultivating optimism, then, isn't about ignoring life's hardships. It's about equipping yourself with the mental frameworks, emotional tools, and social supports that help you navigate these hardships more effectively. By embracing a cheerful, authentic form of positivity, you improve not only your chances of success but also your ability to savor the journey along the way.

12 Importance
Finding Freedom in Detachment

Often, we give things far more importance than they truly deserve. Importance, in many ways, is a form of attachment, one that can distort our perception of what actually matters. In the grand scheme of existence, when we zoom out and consider the vastness of the universe and the inevitability of change, nothing truly matters in an absolute sense. Yet, within our personal microcosmos, such as our immediate lives, relationships, and experiences, we inevitably cast ourselves as the central protagonists. Because of this, everything we do, feel, and think can seem disproportionately important. This perceived importance generates stress, drama, and sometimes deep-seated trauma.

Remember the example of a character in a TV show and the observer watching them? For the character, a particular event may feel monumentally significant, fraught with tension and heartbreak. For you, the distant observer, the exact same scenario is just another plot point, eliciting no real urgency. If we learn to recognize these exaggerated signals of importance, life can become more navigable. By ignoring the compulsion to label every event as crucial, we find that moving forward with calm detachment becomes easier.

Giving too much importance to a belief, an idea, a situation, your job, or even a person means you're hitching your entire sense of self to that thing. Your Children, being the exception, of course, since you're biologically wired to protect them. But for most everything else, it's like wearing a „*Handle With Care*" sticker on your ego. When we tie our identity to something external, letting it go feels less like dropping a bad habit and more like a dramatic scene where part of you is being written out of existence. The ego, whose main gig is keeping you feeling safe and relevant, hates this. So, it kicks, screams, and throws a mental tantrum, creating all kinds of emotional turbulence to stop you from moving on.

Marcus Aurelius had the perfect antidote to this existential drama: „*Think of yourself as dead. You have lived your life. Now take what's left and live it properly.*" Sure, it sounds a bit morbid, but it's a masterclass in detachment. If you've already „*died*" to the things you're clinging to, you stop acting like they're the keys to your survival. Maybe, just maybe, it's time to let an outdated version of yourself die today. The one clinging to that job title, that toxic relationship, or that belief you've outgrown.

Now, let's be real: there are exceptions. Your kid's health? Definitely worth prioritizing. But most other things? Probably not worth the emotional stranglehold. Loosening your grip on what you've declared „*important*" is like cutting the chains on a self-imposed prison of anxiety. It's oddly freeing. And sometimes, life throws you a curveball that forces this perspective shift, like surfers who almost drown in the ocean. They'll tell you that coming face-to-face with the raw power of nature is terrifying, sure, but also humbling. It's the ultimate ego-check, a visceral reminder that you are not, in fact, the universe's VIP.

Of course, nobody's asking you to become a Zen master overnight and ditch all attachments. But every now and then, it's worth stepping back and asking: „*Is this really worth my mental energy?*" Most of the time, you'll find the answer is no. Reducing the importance of things doesn't mean you stop caring; it just means you stop treating every bump in the road like it's the end of the highway. That way, you stay adaptable, ready to pivot when a path dead-ends or a better route appears.

Let's talk about work, the thing we're all told to pursue with vigor, like it's some sacred quest. Now, imagine taking that importance dial and turning it down a few notches. What if your current job wasn't the be-all and end-all of your existence? Suddenly, a bad day at work wouldn't feel like the opening scene of a Shakespearean tragedy. That botched presentation—Not a death sentence. And those tense wage negotiations—Just a slightly awkward dance, not a gladiator match where your survival is at stake.

When you stop equating your worth with your job title, the world becomes less terrifying and a lot more interesting. You realize, „*Hey, I've got skills! Transferable ones! I can take this show on the road!*" That realization is liberating because it frees you to pivot without spiraling into an existential crisis. Maybe you even look up from your email for the first time in years and notice that your current job isn't leading anywhere fulfilling. It's just a hamster wheel with fancier jargon. Reducing its importance doesn't mean slacking off; it means zooming out and realizing there's a whole buffet of opportunities out there. And no, you're not stuck with the sad salad you've been nibbling on for years. Go ahead, grab a slice of pizza from life's career table.

It is crucial to note that reducing importance does not mean reducing your efforts or aspirations. I once struggled with severe anxiety during my university exams. My fears about the future fueled my study habits but hampered my performance during the tests themselves, turning them into ordeals. It was only in my last semester, after my father passed away, that I gained a sobering perspective on what truly mattered. This loss taught me that my terror over hypothetical futures was both irrational and unproductive. While fear might occasionally push us past certain obstacles, it often cripples us when the critical moment arrives. By accepting my fear, acknowledging its irrationality, and not allowing it to balloon the significance of exams, I found a calmer mindset in which to perform, unburdened by the suffocating weight of excessive importance.

12.1 Confidence Without Clinging

The sense of importance induces anxiety. The more we listen to the ego's proclamations that this or that event is crucial, the more we feel threatened. We become more confident and stable by quieting this inner voice and choosing not to believe every urgent whisper of importance. Think of a truly confident person. They tend to remain peaceful under stress. To them, the supposedly „huge" issue is just another aspect of life to navigate. From the outside, it might look like a remarkable display of composure, but from their internal vantage point, the situation simply isn't inflated with undue importance. This difference in perception can transform a tense ordeal into a manageable Tuesday afternoon. A lack of confidence often stems from over-importance: we inflate the weight of challenges until they become paralyzing. If we want our ego to assist us rather than sabotage us, we must ensure not to feed it with excessive importance.

There are countless approaches to improving confidence. One effective way is to imagine life as a movie or a game, where you merely observe the main character—yourself—without merging your identity with their struggles. As spectators, we clearly see what might harm the protagonist, yet we watch without panic because we know there's a broader storyline at play. Once we stop identifying so strongly with the character's immediate dramas, we can maintain emotional equilibrium. Another way is to gather irrefutable evidence of our competence. When our mind accepts that we are indeed skilled, confidence emerges more naturally. It's also helpful to understand when fear or guilt is playing a role.

Sometimes, the absence of confidence is merely the presence of unfounded fear or a belief in our lack of skill.

Cut yourself and others some slack. Life isn't an audition for a superhero team. Everyone's just trying to figure out how to get through their own blooper reel. Challenges that once felt monumental no longer hold the same weight as we accumulate experience and resilience. Over time, each new trial appears less important than the last.

A useful shortcut to confidence is allowing yourself to have shortcomings. By adjusting the weight you place on your own skills, and even on your flaws, you free yourself from the need to posture or overcompensate. If you judge others harshly while harboring insecurities about your own abilities, it might indicate you are trying to mask your own perceived inadequacies. Such defensiveness can make you an unpleasant companion.

Instead, forgive yourself for your imperfections and learn to let go of the rigid self-image you cling to. Overemphasizing your shortcomings only proves that they remain disproportionately important in your mind. If someone tries to mock or judge you based on these flaws, you won't be wounded because your ego no longer interprets their words as a threat. This emotional freedom allows the conversation to continue naturally. Ironically, it may even earn you more respect as people recognize your grounded self-assurance. On the other hand, taking your flaws and achievements too seriously endangers your self-worth, leaving you fragile before others' judgments.

We all assign importance to certain circumstances as part of our internal ordering system. This is normal and even necessary for prioritization. However, giving too much importance disrupts the delicate balance. While external pressures may tempt you into magnifying the significance of events, ultimately, it's an internal decision. Sometimes, you choose this inflation consciously, but more often, it happens subconsciously. When you ruminate incessantly about problems, your mind treats them as urgent matters, reinforcing their gravity. Constant mental chatter about an issue magnifies it, making it seem insurmountable. But in truth, this wall is constructed by our own minds. A quiet mind is peaceful, and a peaceful mind is confident, even when confronting challenges. Achieving that quietness often involves stepping back and asking: „*Is this really as critical as I've made it out to be?*"

12.2 When Expression becomes Obsession

Many people believe that talking about your problems helps solve them. While verbalizing issues can offer temporary relief and create a sense of security in vulnerability, it doesn't necessarily solve the underlying problem. Sharing your troubles may feel comforting, like having a safe space to be heard, but it can also reinforce the belief that these problems are immense and pressing. Hale Dwoskin succinctly captured this idea: „*The only reason we want to understand our problems is because we are planning to have them again.*" By repeatedly discussing a problem, we find more evidence of its severity. Confirmation bias takes hold, and our conversation partners often conform to our viewpoint to offer support, thereby solidifying the problem's importance.

This dynamic can make certain forms of therapy or support groups tricky. While many therapists are skilled professionals who can genuinely help, there are situations where the therapeutic context itself encourages a cycle of temporary relief followed by dependency. It becomes like a drug, a temporary feeling of security and self-worth that fades once the session ends, leaving you feeling more entrenched in victimhood. In some circles, people even begin to identify with therapy itself, boasting more about having gone to therapy than about the insights gained therein.

Therapists are like a GPS for your mind. They can guide you, but you're still the one driving. No app will magically teleport you to happiness. The same can be said for those who rely solely on psychedelic experiences or external tools. While these can provide meaningful glimpses into the workings of the mind, they do not replace the inner work necessary for lasting change. A trained professional can absolutely assist you in severing the emotional charge from painful memories, helping you approach your problems from a calmer vantage point. But the realizations must come from within.

This leads us to an essential truth: both professional guidance and introspective experiences can be powerful tools to learn more about yourself, but the genuine realization and the transformative action must arise internally. You are the one who must decide to act on these insights. There is no prince in shining armor, no ultimate savior who will ride in and solve all your problems. Those who claim they can magically fix everything for you usually have their own agendas. True change and deep understanding emanate from taking responsibility for your own journey, facing your burdens without inflating them into towering monsters of importance. By recognizing that importance is something we ascribe, not something that inherently exists, you gain the freedom to sculpt a more peaceful, flexible, and confident inner life.

Ultimately, acknowledging that importance is often a self-created mirage can liberate you from the grip of unnecessary stress and help you live more authentically.

13 Love and Relationships
Redefining Connections and Self-Love

What is love, really? We use the word „*love*" so casually in our society that it risks losing its essence. We say we „*love*" a particular dish, „*love*" a TV show, or even claim „*love*" for nearly everything that brings us pleasure. We love a lot, don't we? Or do we, in fact, love too little? One might wonder if our collective understanding of love has become so fragmented that defining it proves surprisingly difficult.

Why is this so? For starters, love demands the awareness and attention of a conscious being. Without awareness, love cannot exist. It is not a simple reflex, nor just a biochemical cocktail. Yet even when we acknowledge love as a state of conscious feeling, we must accept that it also has physiological roots. The famous phrase „*butterflies in your stomach*" turns out to be more accurate than we might imagine: our autonomic nervous system, the „*little brain*" in the heart (the intrinsic cardiac nervous system), and our gut, where much of our serotonin is produced, all play roles. Although the complex orchestration of love occurs largely in our brains, our bodies provide the theater and the props.

Yet this intrinsic event we call love is the foundation for all the relationships in human society. From the person you plan to stay with for the rest of your life to the person just passing by, you will feel varying degrees of love. The feeling is not based on your logical faculties, but it dictates a huge part of our actions.

To better understand the word „*love*," it would perhaps have been helpful to have different words for it, like the Greeks did. I already broke the taboo previously to claim that love had conditions. The first and most relevant condition is that it requires us to be selfless, though to varying degrees. For all the fairies and pixies out there, no need to despair on this conundrum; everything is still love. It is just a matter of perspective. Assuming our natural state is selflessness and love, then conditions in their selfish nature separate us from it.

In a more recent approach, John Alan Lee tried to expand on the Greek approach to describing love by categorizing it into primary and secondary types for greater precision and richness. The primary types are:

- **Eros**, which stands for passionate and romantic love, driven by physical attraction and desire.

- **Ludus**, representing playful, game-playing love, characterized by casual and uncommitted interactions.
- **Storge**, an affectionate, friendship-based love, built on long-term familiarity and emotional closeness.

These primary types blend to form secondary types:

- **Pragma**, emerging from Ludus and Storge, is logical and practical love, based on compatibility and shared goals.
- **Mania**, arising from Eros and Ludus, is obsessive and possessive love, fueled by high intensity and emotional volatility.
- **Agape**, combining Eros and Storge, is selfless and altruistic love, given freely without any conditions.

Given that we are now better equipped to describe love, we can see that there is unconditional love in the form of Agape, a love to God, the universe, or humanity. Some will even be as devoted to their partner, sacrificing everything for the relationship. Which, as we know, is not always for the better, depending on the partner. It is a form of love that almost comes with a certain amount of naivety. It comes deep from the heart, and the mind does not interfere. It is a blissful and exciting state to be in. In a sense, it is the opposite of suffering. Suffering is a form of selfishness where the ego jumps in to rescue us from perceived harm. While we know too well that this is not always helpful, it is still a good self-preservation strategy, given that some people don't mean well. These varied expressions of love take root early in life, shaping how we connect and protect ourselves.

From our earliest relationships, the ones that first cracked our hearts open and taught us how vulnerable we really are, any disruption feels like a catastrophe. When these bonds are shaken, we don't just lose trust; we lose our wide-eyed innocence, that glorious sense of naivety that made the world feel safe. Instead, we're left wounded, caught in a spiral of self-doubt and unhealthy patterns, wearing the invisible label of „damaged." We allowed an external event to take control of our internal world. This was the greatest tragedy of life. This is the moment the ego is born, our inner bodyguard. It steps in, builds walls, and says, „Don't worry, I've got this. I'll keep you safe." And it does, for a time. It helps us set boundaries, defend ourselves, and survive. But while the ego shields us from harm, it also cages us, stealing our freedom and that divine birthright to live in a constant state of love.

Validation, comfort, and safety: these are precisely the promises our ego makes. When love becomes mixed up with these needs, it turns into something transactional, a subtle exchange rather than a freely flowing energy. Often, when we say we love someone, we're unconsciously asking them to validate our worth, comfort our pain, or guarantee our emotional safety. But is this love, or just fear in disguise?

True love does not seek; it simply is. It emerges effortlessly when we stop needing our partners or anyone else to heal wounds that can only ever be healed from within.

Thankfully, all is not lost. With time and devotion, we can reclaim that state, having learned not to hand over our hearts blindly to anyone or anything except life itself. My advice: live like a wise fool—someone who's seen the depths but still chooses to dance on the cliff. That's how you get the most out of this wild ride.

13.1 Love Begins Within

As we examine our earliest attachments, we must recognize how validation, comfort, and safety shape our patterns. The way we received or lacked these things in childhood determines how desperately we seek them in adulthood. Only when we consciously become the source of our own validation, comfort, and safety do we free our partners from the impossible responsibility of fulfilling unmet childhood needs. This, in turn, liberates our relationships, transforming them from struggles for reassurance into genuine partnerships rooted in freedom and mutual appreciation.

What we perceive as love is highly influenced by our parents, and they might have had their own screwed idea about love. We will find people treating us similarly to how our parents treated each other. Therefore, people with narcissistic parents will often seek out a person with the same traits, as this is our understanding of love. According to John Bowlby, our early relationship with our caregivers shapes our patterns of attachment:

- **Secure Attachment**: Characterized by trust, a positive view of oneself and others, and healthy relationships. Securely attached individuals tend to have fulfilling and stable relationships.

- **Anxious Attachment**: Characterized by a preoccupation with relationships, fear of abandonment, and often needy or clingy behavior. Individuals with an anxious attachment style may experience anxiety and insecurity in their relationships.

- **Avoidant Attachment**: Characterized by a discomfort with closeness and dependence on others. Avoidant individuals often maintain emotional distance and may struggle with intimacy and commitment.

This represents in no way what love is, but rather what our internal needs are to feel loved, projecting our internal needs with our behavior patterns onto our partner. While I am advocating unconditional love to the world. It is unreasonable to assume that this is possible in our daily relationships. Sure, some spiritual Guru will say they achieved that state of enlightenment. But the skeptic within us might rightfully always be asking if he is just a trickster. In our daily relationships, we mostly have conditional relationships. Could you feel loved by your romantic partner if they were just giving out their romantic love to anyone like candy?

But even in the model from John Alan Lee, we find that different variations of attachments play a big role, from the purest form of love, in the form of Agape, to an obsessive relationship in the form of Mania. Risking sounding like an avoidantly attached person here, if we become more attached to the thing we love, the more we suppress our love. We become so attached to the concept of love that we forget to be in love. At this point, it is not love, but an attachment.

I will lend the words of Abraham Twerski: „Love is a word that, in our culture, has almost lost its meaning. Let me tell you a story about the Rabi of Kursk. He came across a young man who was clearly enjoying a dish of fish that he was eating, and he said: 'Young man, why are you eating that fish?'. And the young man says, 'Because I love fish!'. He says: 'Oh, you love the fish, that's why you took it out of the water and killed it and boiled it.' He said, 'Don't tell me you love the fish; you love yourself, and because the fish tastes good to you, therefore you took it out of the water and killed it, and boiled it.' So much of what is love is fish-love."

It describes how we confuse the obsession with ourselves, this fevering mania, with the freedom of true love. Note how I do not call it self-love. Love is fleeting, and by holding on to it, you will only crush it. But if you are not attached to the person you love but can be in love together, then you are in a state of love. This state of non-attachment can only exist if you are willing to let go. If you like a butterfly, you don't hold onto it, as it will crush the butterfly. You will let it land on your knee, and if it feels comfortable, it will stay or come back. As Thich Nhat Hanh, the Buddhist monk, says, *„You must love in such a way that the person you love feels free."*

There is only one relationship that lasts your entire life: the relationship with yourself. Mastering this relationship is no easy task, but it is perhaps the most profound one to master, as your inner affairs project outward, defining your relationship with the world. When we start observing our thoughts, we might find that our relationship with ourselves is not very loving. Would you speak to another person the same way you talk to yourself? True love can only be expressed through freedom, and desires are the shackles to that freedom. When your mind does what it needs, not what it desires, you become a free person.

The most toxic people can be good company if they're happy. By labeling them as toxic, we perpetuate the „*us vs. them*" mentality, failing to recognize that we can be toxic, too, when we're unhappy. Have you ever noticed that some people seem to live in a magical world while others are trapped in a cursed one? The world is just a mirror of their inner state. If you believe the world is out to get you, it will be. But if you believe the universe has your back, that will be true, too. Neither the enchanted nor the bewitched can change the world around them; they simply reflect it. So, let's not focus on how people can be toxic to each other but rather on how we can be toxic to ourselves.

One way we can be toxic to ourselves is through our choice of partners. Our bodies respond to people who are in a similar state of mind as ours, often unconsciously. We can literally sense their levels of stress. Choosing partners with similar stress levels can lead to smoother conversations and a more familiar form of suffering. Marie-Louise von Franz suggests that women who have not discovered their animus choose men who have not discovered their anima, and vice versa. Such relationships are often labeled as toxic. It doesn't matter if you call your partner toxic, avoidant, or narcissistic; what matters is recognizing that we must resolve our internal separations. It's not about what our partner has done to us, but about our illusions of the world. Tactics like gaslighting, emotional blackmail, guilt-tripping, and constant criticism only work if we are disconnected from ourselves. The narcissist needs the codependent, and vice versa. The gap between the outward presentation and the internal reality causes this disconnection. If you find yourself in such a relationship and are an adult, you always have the option to leave.

13.2 Facing Rejection: The Doorway to True Connection

Have you ever stood trembling at the edge of a moment? Heart hammering against your ribs, palms slick with sweat, the simple act of stepping forward feels like a leap off a cliff. Maybe it was bearing your soul, asking for what you crave, or reaching out to bridge the gap between you and another. That razor-sharp edge, slicing through your courage, is the fear of rejection. It's a shadow we all know, yet it stabs each of us in an achingly personal way.

Why does rejection hit us so hard? Science has an answer that'll make you wince: a study in PNAS found that social rejection lights up the same brain regions as a punch to the face or a broken bone. Our bodies don't just feel it, they scream it, registering exclusion as a primal threat to survival. It's a relic of our ancient past when getting cast out of the tribe wasn't just lonely. It was a death sentence. No wonder a „no" can twist in your gut like an emotional dagger, leaving you raw and reeling.

And yet, here's the kicker: rejection's grip on us isn't fixed. It's a force we can wrestle with, a beast we can tame or even befriend. Whether it shackles us in silence or flings open the door to freedom depends on how we choose to meet it.

Until my mid-twenties, talking to women wasn't just intimidating. It was a personal apocalypse. Every imagined rejection ballooned into a nightmare: *She'll laugh. She'll sneer. She'll see right through me.* I'd rehearse conversations in my head like a desperate actor, scripting every word, every pause, hoping perfection would armor me against judgment. But all that mental choreography? It usually ended with me frozen, lips sealed, suffocating in a cage of my own making. Sure, it is safe, but utterly miserable.

Then life threw me a lifeline in the form of Martin and Farid, two friends who saw through my self-imposed prison bars. They knew avoiding rejection wasn't protecting me. It was choking me. So, they took it upon themselves to nudge me out, sometimes with a gentle shove, sometimes with a smirk and a dare. On nights out, they'd lean in, eyes glinting with mischief: „Go talk to her. What's the worst that could happen? She'll sprout fangs and eat you?" At first, it felt like torture. My stomach churning, my legs lead-heavy. But their playful, unshakable confidence was a slow drip of courage I couldn't ignore.

Those first stumbles were a mess. Awkward silences, stammered words, one spectacular flop where I tripped over my own feet mid-sentence. But something wild happened: each rejection I survived didn't break me. It built me. Each cringe-worthy moment chipped away at the monster in my mind. Neuroscience backs this up with cold, hard facts: studies on exposure therapy show that repeatedly facing what terrifies you, whether it's heights, spiders, or a stranger's „no," rewires your brain, dialing down the panic. With every rejection, my dread softened into a spark of curiosity: *What happens next?* Instead of a gut punch, it started feeling like a step up.

This isn't just my story. It's the premise of **Rejection Therapy**: a brilliant experiment Jia Jiang turned into a viral quest. He spent 100 days chasing „*no's,*" asking strangers for outrageous things like borrowing $100 or piloting a plane, to desensitize himself to rejection's sting. What he uncovered was mind-blowing: rejection wasn't the personal attack he'd feared. Most times, it was about the other person's day, their mood, their baggage, but not about him. The terror melted into something lighter, even laughable. I found the same truth. A woman brushing me off didn't mean I was worthless. It might've meant she was late, distracted, or just not in the mood. Rejection stopped being a mirror of my soul and became a window into someone else's.

Here's where it gets juicy: the perks of facing rejection spill far beyond pickup lines or barstool chats. It's a masterclass in living bolder. It teaches you to:

- **Courage to act**, unshackled from fear's paralysis.
- **Emotional resilience**, dulling the sting of needing approval.
- **Clearer communication**, honed by risking directness.
- **Creative freedom**, unburdened by dread of a shutdown.
- **Inner strength**, keeping you steady amid life's turbulence.
- **A new success metric**, where effort trumps outcomes.

But wait, there's more to this than toughness. Rejection's got a secret soft side. Ever notice how a „no" can feel like a dodged bullet? That job that didn't call back, that date who ghosted, that friend who drifted, sometimes rejection's a cosmic favor, steering you away from a mismatch. A woman turning me down once stung like

186

hell, but months later, I'd see it: *Thank God.* She wasn't my pace, my vibe, my truth. The same goes for life's bigger gambles, like careers, collaborations, or dreams. A slammed door might just mean it's not *your* door. The universe, in its messy way, is nudging you toward one that is.

Intrigued yet? Here's a tidbit to chew on: psychologists say rejection can even spark creativity. A 2012 study from Johns Hopkins found that people who'd faced social rejection often came up with more original ideas afterward. Maybe because they stopped caring so much about fitting in. Rejection doesn't just toughen you; it can unshackle your mind.

So, how do you dive in? You don't need to storm the castle. Just dip your toes into the uncomfortable. Try these:

- Ask for a discount at a shop, even if the price tag's set in stone.
- Tell a stranger their funky hat looks like it's from a sci-fi flick.
- Ask a barista to whip up a drink they invent on the spot.
- Throw your hat in the ring for a gig you're half-qualified for.
- Post a hot take online—unfiltered, unapologetic, you.

The point isn't to rack up rejections like trophies. It's to face the fear that's kept your voice small. Every „*no*" is a badge of honor because it means you showed up. You swung the bat. You lived.

As rejection lost its fangs, something magical unfolded: my connections got real. I stopped tiptoeing around, fishing for validation, and started showing up as me, with flaws, quirks, all of it. Conversations turned into playgrounds, not battlegrounds, whether I was chatting up a stranger or catching up with a friend. Martin and Farid, with their laughter and dares, didn't just push me, they freed me. Looking back, I grin at those shaky first steps, grateful for the guts to move despite the tremble.

The irony's almost poetic: run from rejection, and you stay stuck; embrace it, and you soar. Fear shrinks, confidence blooms, and relationships turn honest. Brené Brown's research on vulnerability nails it by stating that risking rejection isn't optional for connection; it's the price of admission. You've got to wade through the muck of „*maybe not*" to reach the gold of „*yes, this is real.*"

Rejection isn't the enemy we've made it out to be. It's a guide, a compass, pointing us toward what fits. The sting fades fast, but the freedom? That's forever. So I dare you: step onto that wobbly edge. Dance with rejection. It's not just a risk—it's a revelation.

13.3 Reclaiming Your Space

While I detest self-indulgence in my suffering, my family provides an exceptional example to illustrate the concept of drama. By writing this, I may summon another hurricane of chaos, as some family members hold their personas in high regard. Any attack on these personas is seen as an existential threat, justifying any form of retribution. One of my siblings, driven by hope for change, did the unthinkable, creating a conflict that lasted six years, involving four lawsuits and countless stressful encounters. When Kali unleashes her wrath on sinners, she could learn a thing or two from my family.

The dynamic we'll dissect here is drama. We all know it too well and have been entangled in these toxic tendrils. According to Stephen Karpman, there are three roles in a drama:

- **Victim**: The person who feels oppressed, helpless, and powerless. They often seek sympathy and support from others but don't take responsibility for their own circumstances.
- **Persecutor**: The person who blames, criticizes, and dominates. They often assert power and control over others, making the Victim feel oppressed.
- **Rescuer**: The person who intervenes to help or save the Victim, often without being asked. They derive satisfaction from feeling needed but can also perpetuate the Victim's helplessness.

My oldest brother, like a dutiful first-born son of the family, did what was expected and took over the farm. In a sense, he and I are opposites: he always tried to do the right thing, though confined by his belief systems, while I am the black sheep of the family, leaving my religious circle, going raving, trying mind-altering substances, exploring spiritual practices, and fighting for my right not to be used as child labor. There is still envy about the perception that I worked less on the farm, ignoring the fact that I fought bloody hard for it. But what a burden of a child I must have been. In a sense, it was lucky that there was a certain neglect, granting me freedom in that process. With five children, one lost still leaves four, no? I didn't burden my family with my problems or adventures, not because I didn't want a tribe, but because I knew early on that sharing my hardships would bring no good. Most of them will learn about my life for the first time through this book.

While drama is not unusual in my family, my brother, in his foolishness and religious conviction, assumed the role of the rescuer. Let's just say that the way of communication that my mother is used to is very direct. Her entire existence is about survival and work, which means that anything you do that does not fit into that lens is blasphemy. One of the cashiers didn't clean during a lull, throwing my mother into a rage. After her stroke, she learned to handle such situations more calmly.

My brother was not aware of David Emerald's work at the time, and let me be honest, probably this did not change. So, he did what a good Christian would do: he stood up as a savior. He assumed the role of the rescuer, making my mother the persecutor and the cashier the victim. Now, to his demise, he did what Karpman describes as role shifting and told my mother that she could not work on the farm she built with my father. Making him the persecutor and my mother the victim. When we are entangled with people that cause drama, then the roles will constantly shift. While we might believe that there is at least some nobility in being the victim or the rescuer, it could not be further from the truth. In drama-laden relationships, roles constantly shift, and staying in this dynamic means we eventually become perpetrators.

Now, more than six years have passed, and the conflict is still raging. However, at this point, one of my sisters joined in, acting as a rescuer in the pursuit of finally gaining my mother's approval. But while my mother is hot-tempered, this specific sister is ill-tempered. Besides daily conflicts, there are two lawsuits related to physical harm and one lawsuit to reclaim the farm he inherited. Besides a lot of effort to destroy his character, he still maintained his good name. The actors in the drama need to reaffirm their roles, and they are codependent on each other. Otherwise, the drama would fail, which would be devastating, as at this point, there is an identification that happened. I hope, my dear reader, that you are not in a situation like this, but if you are, then you need to learn fast how to set your boundaries and remove yourself physically from the situation.

If Jesus knew David Emerald's work, he probably would not have chosen to become a savior but a coach instead. Emerald proposes the following roles to foster healthier interactions:

- **Creator** (instead of Victim): Focuses on outcomes and solutions, taking responsibility for their actions and choices.
- **Challenger** (instead of Persecutor): Encourages and inspires others to grow, pushing them to achieve their potential in a supportive way.
- **Coach** (instead of Rescuer): Helps others to find their solutions and supports them in their journey without taking over.

What hypocrisy to preach about unconditional love and a second later talk about cutting people out of your life. But true self-love also means that you need to set boundaries on how people can interact with you. As we embark on the journey of reconnecting with our true selves, it is fundamental. Your ego will only be quiet if you truly believe that its primary function to keep you safe is covered. You cannot be truly safe with toxic relationships in your life. At this point, I will not waste a single breath and take immediate action to distance myself from an individual perpetrating drama, even if it means significant loss.

The most important relationship we need to nurture is the relationship with ourselves. At the same time, many people will experience toxic relationships only temporarily and towards a single person, if at all. We surprisingly never realize that we are constantly in such relationships with the world, especially with the groups we are in.

14 Group Dynamics
Breaking Free from the Collective Hallucination

Many of the topics mentioned before were foreplay to make this chapter as lubricating as possible. Groups hold so much more weight than most are aware of, and freeing the mind from this restraint is not an easy task. But understand that I speak from a place of love, though I question some of your deeply held beliefs in this chapter. This journey begins by recognizing how our surroundings subtly shape our thoughts and actions.

You will find that your environment will not always like it if you are changing. This is inherent in all of us, as the other person becomes harder to predict. One of the main functions of the brain is predicting the future to secure survival. But we are running with badly written and outdated software, preventing us from thinking objectively and rationally. Especially when it comes to the groups we are in. Think of their confusion as an error message: „*Does not compute! Go back to the old version!*" This does not mean that you should now leave your social support system. But in our blissful ignorance, we are painfully unaware of how much we are influenced by the groups we are in.

14.1 How Groups Influence Us

The psychological experiments conducted in the last century are witness to this human design error. The Milgram experiment, conducted in the 1960s, starkly illustrates how group dynamics and authority figures can profoundly influence our behavior, affecting both minor actions and significant decisions. Participants, instructed by an authority figure to administer increasingly painful electric shocks to another person, often complied despite the apparent distress of the recipient. This willingness to obey, even when it conflicts with personal morals, highlights how social pressure and the presence of authority can lead individuals to act in ways they might not otherwise consider. The experiments demonstrate that our behavior is not only shaped by major societal norms and commands but also by everyday interactions and subtle cues from those around us. Whether conforming to group decisions in a meeting or following societal rules, the influence of others is a powerful force in guiding our actions. Such experiments reveal just one facet of how groups mold us, with conformity playing an equally powerful role.

Another example illustrating how we conform to our environment is shown by Solomon Asch. The Asch conformity experiments, conducted in the 1950s, revealed how group pressure can lead individuals to conform even against their own judgment. Participants were asked to match the length of a line with one of three comparison lines, as illustrated below, in the presence of a group that intentionally chose incorrect answers. Remarkably, many participants conformed to the group's wrong choices, demonstrating the powerful influence of social pressure. This experiment highlights how individuals often conform to group norms to fit in, avoid conflict, or doubt their own perceptions, illustrating the strong impact of group dynamics on personal behavior.

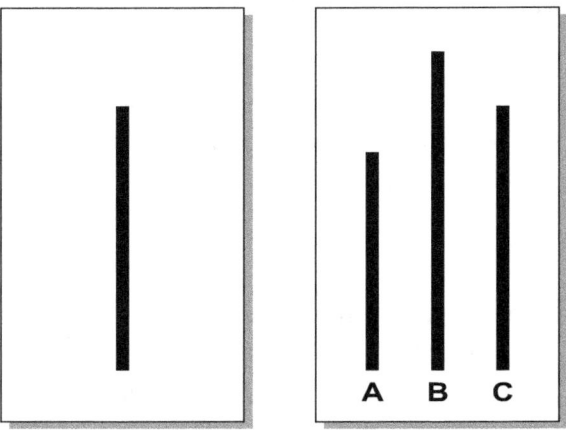

Figure 1: https://en.wikipedia.org/wiki/File:Asch_experiment.svg

But it cannot be this bad, right? The Stanford prison experiment, led by Philip Zimbardo in 1971, illustrated how situational factors and assigned roles can drastically alter individuals' behavior. Participants were randomly assigned to be either guards or prisoners in a simulated prison environment. The *„guards"* quickly adopted authoritarian behaviors, becoming increasingly abusive, while the *„prisoners"* became passive and submissive. This experiment underscores how groups and assigned roles can influence behavior, often leading individuals to act in ways they might not in other contexts. The experiment had to be terminated before it ended due to safety concerns. It reveals the influence of our environment and our role in that environment. The adoption of the roles was astonishingly fast. Shaping the actions of the participants and sometimes resulting in extreme behaviors that aligned with perceived group norms and expectations.

While this error of our behavior casts a detrimental light upon human nature, we can make some use of our shortcomings. If we surround ourselves with people who are relentless in their pursuit of improving themselves and the world, then it will be very likely that we will also conform. This also means the opposite, and the people around us can pull us down. Our environment has the biggest impact on our paths. If our environment is influencing our behavior, we can make use of that by influencing our environment. Otherwise, any conscious effort we make to improve will be backbreaking. Find people who are on the same journey; otherwise, the path of self-transformation will be as challenging as Sisyphus's eternal punishment of rolling a stone uphill.

14.2 Harmony and Disharmony

Even with just one other person, the dynamic shifts. If it is only a group with two people, you might call it a relationship, and you can identify the status of said relationship. But way too often, we do not consider that there is also a relationship with the entity, which is represented by a group. But you are in a relationship with these nonphysical entities, and it is up to you to identify if the status of this relationship is beneficial or toxic for you. The life force of these entities is human attention. If there is no attention put into a group, it will vanish. The best way to have a constant flow of attention is by having an ideology to identify with because if there is no concept of self, then your nation, friends, family, politics, or religion can give you a sense of self. Some might argue that the highest form of self can also only be achieved by serving a greater good.

„I say the world must learn of our peaceful ways... by force!" — Bender Bending Rodriguez in Futurama.

There has probably been done more harm in the name of a greater good than there has been done good. The problem is not the greater good but what we identify as such. Serving a greater good can only be achieved when we are at inner peace. Inner peace, however, cannot be achieved if we are still dancing to the tunes of entities outside of us.

„If there is to be peace in the world,
There must be peace in the nations.

If there is to be peace in the nations,
There must be peace in the cities.

If there is to be peace in the cities,
There must be peace between neighbors.

If there is to be peace between neighbors,
There must be peace in the home.

If there is to be peace in the home,
There must be peace in the heart."

—Lao-Tsu

To be in harmony with the world will be fundamental to uncovering our true selves. It is not that we must find our true self, as it has never left us. But rather, we must uncover it by peeling away all the layers of identification. This is a painful process, as initially, it will feel as if we are losing ourselves because what are we if we do not have a way of identifying? But you will find that once the layers are removed, they are not a protective armor against the world but a prison holding you in place.

For humans, being part of a group is vital. We are, after all, herd animals. Having a close-knit community provides comfort and security. By playing or talking with other people, we can create a flow state very easily. The cooperation that happens in groups allows us to create things that would have been far outside of our grasp as individuals. Having this dynamic going on allowed us to become the top predator on this planet. Most importantly, a group gives us a sense of security. It's a beautiful part of being human that we're not solitary, like polar bears. We have vibrant cultures that have evolved from this desire to be in groups.

It could be argued that modern society has not found a proper mechanism to cover this need to be part of a community. Churches provide this sense, but after we became secular, no alternative was presented. Other than sports clubs, not many options come to mind. Most communities are hardly accessible, with many having obscure conditions for membership. Take fraternities and the military, for example. They often have hazing rituals that require you to sacrifice your dignity from the get-go. In other groups, you must spend a lot of money or time to belong. Instead of realizing we've lost something, we even become proud and elitist about our groups. Many people spend fortunes at clubs to show how exclusive they are. But this status only matters to those caught in the same desires. Someone who doesn't care for bottle service might even pity the person who ordered one.

14.3 Entanglement by Desires

Hell is real! But it's *not* some underground sauna for sinners. It happens in the eternal now, and it resonates with your dissonance of the world. All dissonance arises from unmet expectations, which are rooted in our beliefs about the world. Beliefs are heuristics for predictions. When these beliefs are threatened, we experience fear, and when they are violated, we feel guilt. Fear represents a lack of safety, while guilt reflects unmet expectations, both signaling a perceived deficiency. Historically, these emotions served as survival mechanisms to drive change. But we do not have to fight sabretooth tigers for resources anymore, yet many people are in a constant state of lack.

If you observe your environment, you will find that this is artificially created. Due to the feeling of lack, a feeling of incompleteness, and therefore, desires are born. Due to your newfound desires, it is possible to sell you a product or an idea. Unaware of this internal process, we assume that external solutions endorsed by others can fix what we perceive as wrong. You will find that this feeling of lack creates a separation within. If this state persists, it causes suffering. Yet in nature, fear is not a lasting state. But in our society, marketing and groups use it to create a constant state of separation.

Many might never experience inner peace, having been conditioned by an initial group, typically their family. Assuming that the world operates by these states, adapting to it and perpetuating it onto others. A cycle of unconscious abuse, not to be broken by generations.

Groups require constant attention from their adherents. Otherwise, the group will vanish. Therefore, a common ideology is relevant for groups that survived throughout generations. Our friends, for example, are hopefully a group not based on beliefs, but once the last person withdraws their attention, the group dissolves. This creates an incentive for groups to capture and retain attention. If your goal were to start a cult, mastering the manipulation of attention would be essential. On the contrary, this means you need to become aware of where you put your attention!

Not only do we inherit shame from our parents, but it is also force-fed by society through marketing, religion, and politics. Women are shamed for having too much sex, while men are shamed for not having enough. We face shame for our appearance, skin color, gender, sexuality, education, and socio-economic status. One side shames us for having too little, the other for having too much. Sadly, shaming and guilt are potent tools for changing human behavior on a large scale, yet on an individual level, they cause great suffering, making us more selfish in the process.

Love is selfless and makes us feel connected. Meanwhile, shame and guilt are cries for love, but they are wrongfully expressed. Tragically, in our selfishness, we create a bitter cycle, trying to shame and guilt-trip those we perceive as more privileged. This behavior is also seen in narcissists. Trauma, often caused by a lack of attention from caregivers before memories can form, leads them to feel inadequate. Any criticism can trigger deep feelings of inadequacy, leading to explosive reactions in overt narcissists or intrigue in covert narcissists. What we perceive as love is a connection to the source, but shame and guilt cut this connection. Our inherent need for love becomes fetishized into a desire for love. However, our perceived lack of love is nothing but an illusion. Originating from the belief that we are separated from the rest of the universe.

Fear, shame, and guilt are powerful tools to capture your attention. Some groups will literally invent something to fear, and the only way you can get a feeling of security back is by joining them. Fear is such a strong emotion that it will override our logical capabilities. The mind will find evidence of why our newfound belief is true, regardless of the facts. All it needs is to plant the seed of fear. While it is easy to implement the belief, letting go of it turns out to be much harder. After all, we have evidence for our belief now. If you have ever been in a situation where you had to let go of one of your core beliefs, you can count yourself lucky.

While it might have been painful at the time, it makes you more flexible in predicting the future. Having to let go of your way of identifying is never fun because who are you, if not this? But eventually, if you give up enough times, the layers you thought were you, you will find a pleasant surprise of an unshakable truth of your innermost core. It is up to you to answer Charles Bukowski's question, *„Can you remember who you were before the world told you who you should be?"* Once that shift happens, it will not make any sense as to why you would define yourself. The question of self-worth will never arise again, as it will not make sense at that point.

It is very easy for us to identify damaging groups for another person. You might have friends or family members who have different political or spiritual beliefs from yours. It becomes even more obvious if you think of people having drug addiction. Maybe you even think of a person right now going down a path that you think is only hurting them. With great effort, you might have even tried to sway their beliefs because you realize that it is harmful to them or others. You might even find that everybody else, other than you, is following the wrong path. You might be surprised to hear that the people you so desperately try to save might think the same about you. This might sound absurd to you. But this is the trap our ego is laying out for us. It makes us ignorant of our own shortcomings.

Consider the case of drug users who relapse after treatment. They have become aware of their bad behavior, but they have not become aware of the source. Take the Vietnam War soldiers, for example. Many used heroin during the war, but when they returned home to a different environment, they stopped. This indicates how much our surroundings dictate our behavior. Even if you recognize a negative pattern, your ego resists change, clinging to familiar people and settings as a survival strategy. But given the abundance of modern times, it is a very bad mechanism. It is very scary for the ego because one version of your ego must die to allow a new version to grow. It might feel like you will have to let go of a part of you.

To survive, we usually must go to work to earn money. Many benefits are coming with this as well. It is our way of contributing to society and feeling a sense of fulfillment. Yet, if you are not totally ignorant, you will have to agree that a certain percentage of your work will not turn into a financial benefit for yourself but for someone else. Your work is an example of such a group. It gives you some benefit for your focused attention, but you do not get the same number of resources back as you generated. If there is compensation happening in the form of companionship, achieving something greater than us, or other good feelings, then there is, in fact, still a fair share of value because generating good experiences is something that we want to maximize. An issue only arises when the compensation is not balanced in relation to the energy we invested. Unless your personal goals align perfectly with the group, you will have to admit that you are working not to fulfill your goals but someone or something else's goals.

This dynamic is true for all groups. To avoid any internal dissonance, our ego, however, will play a trick on us by aligning our goals with the group. It is a self-protection mechanism of our ego to avoid the pain induced by this internal dissonance. Aligning the goals will help us navigate less painfully through life. If a group enhances your experience in exchange for your attention, that's a fair trade. However, many groups are predatory, pretending to have your best interests at heart while exploiting you. Often, it happens under the guise that life is a serious matter after all. Life is meant to be lived, and those who take it too seriously often miss out on feeling truly alive.

14.4 Ideological groups

To control someone, you need to make them feel powerless and dependent on you for help. Many of us willingly give up our responsibilities because they can be burdensome. Handing them over to a group makes us feel lighter, but not freer. True freedom comes from understanding and owning your responsibilities.

Victimhood is the opposite of taking responsibility. You will find two kinds of people claiming to be victims. The ones who haven't yet figured out that they give their power away and are therefore dependent on the whim of others, which pushes them down a road of self-pity and loathing. Only by reclaiming the responsibilities in their life can they regain their independence. Then there is the manipulator, trying to gain something from you, betting on your compassion. Both characters might even tell you that you are a victim as well. While it's true that bad things happen to people, real compassion involves empowering them to reclaim control, not pushing them deeper into self-pity. Remember, what a person takes away from your support is their responsibility, not yours. Feeling guilty only entangles you in a toxic relationship.

Consider North Korea as an extreme case of group manipulation. A system built on fear, where dissent risks not just your life but your family's across generations. There's no revolution or mass exodus, and astonishingly, some even support it, not because they're inherently different from us, but because relentless propaganda has warped their reality. Cults operate similarly, using isolation and repetition to override rational thought, convincing members that the group is their only salvation.

Cognitive therapy, however, offers a counterpoint: it teaches individuals to dissect these imposed beliefs, recognizing them as external distortions rather than personal truths. In politics, we see milder versions, parties stoking fear of „the other" to lock in loyalty. Most supporters aren't sociopaths; they're just caught in a web of manipulation, not unlike the rest of us when we blindly follow group norms.

We all like to think of ourselves as the heroes fighting the evil doers of the world. Our ego likes to think of us as the main character of the story because that is the only way we ever perceive the story. But in reality, we play to the tunes of the groups we are in. Supporting the group grants us resources, but opposing it invites harm. Every group reallocates resources, and while some people benefit, it's naïve to think you'll always be the group's favorite. As you and the world evolve, clashes with the group's norms are inevitable. You then face a choice: submit or face punishment.

This looming threat of punishment triggers feelings of guilt. Violating group rules risks group retribution, which, in our tribal past, often meant death. But what if death isn't something to fear? If it simply means the end of consciousness, then there's no pain to worry about. People who lose their fear of death become harder to control. Yet, our egos are wired to protect our genetic legacy, so threatening our descendants can still induce fear and guilt. Some ideologies even claim that punishment continues after death, reinforcing control through fear.

If this sounds awfully familiar to you and hits you hard, then you probably subscribe to this idea. I went through this experience myself, and probably, this was the first time I became conscious about my inner workings. To break these shackles, you will have to let go. You basically are stuck in a toxic relationship. Your partner always tells you that you are not good enough as you are. You should feel guilty for your sexual desires. He demands constant worship and gets angry if you do not do so. Gaslighting you into beliefs that do not seem to match reality. You should always submit to his command, and anyone who is not on his side is an enemy. And if you do not follow any of these rules, you are an evil sinner.

As a Christian, it was surprisingly easy to point out how ridiculous other religions or sects sounded. But if it comes to our own religion, we do not even dare to question the book. Our ego will put up quite the resistance to push away the pain occurring, which is triggered by these observations. If you are religious yourself, you might feel guilt or even anger because I point them out. After all, you identify as a Christian, Muslim, Buddhist, Hindu, or any other belief. Internally, this will create chaos because who are you if you do not have your religious identification? So much energy was already invested into this specific group, which would all be wasted (Sunk cost fallacy). The ego will create all sorts of stories. It might point us to all the good things the group is doing for us, ignoring all the negative sides, of course. I even told myself a story about how I experienced God due to a nice feeling. It felt like being connected to something. Which, in fact, was not my idea but was suggested by the people of the group, on how to interpret this feeling. I just decided to adopt the story. Now, I can induce similar feelings regularly when meditating without the need for the Abrahamic God.

Smart people are skilled at rationalizing, but this doesn't make their beliefs truer; it just means they're good at deceiving themselves and others. Changing your mind is often seen as a weakness, but it shows adaptability in the face of new evidence. The Dalai Lama exemplifies this with his openness to change: „*If science proves facts that conflict with Buddhist understanding, Buddhism must change accordingly.*" This willingness to adapt is a strength that many Abrahamic religions lack, as they often resist change. For this reason, science was able to fundamentally improve our existence, as we started to change based on new evidence. But the ignorant will sadly claim that a person open to change is untrustworthy. This view is blind to how the world works, as you can only be certain of one thing in the world, which is that the world will change.

If you come to the realization that you can't support the ideologies of your group, then observe your thoughts; do not judge them. Just let them play out and allow yourself to feel the emotions arising. If you give it some time, you might be able to stop giving yourself a label. At the very moment you do not have a label for yourself anymore, you are finally free of the clutches of the group. Instead of identifying with one group, however, you might start identifying with another group. For me, this was atheism and science. While these two groups are more kind masters than the previous ones, they are still very much in control of my reaction to the world. I have many friends who will be ignorant of other experiences because science does not support them. The same will be true if you are diving into the more mystical groups. But if you can let any group be for what it is, without judgment, and mingle, without being entangled, then you will have a broad experience of life.

A clear sign of a toxic group is its tendency to label other groups as evil. Groups can only survive if you put your attention and emotional energy into them. Without your attention, they would vanish, which is an existential threat to any group. At the same time, this means that the members of the group will lose their chance of seeing a different world of different groups. If we travel, we enjoy seeing things that are different from our experience, some of these experiences being our most cherished. It is similar to experiencing different groups. You might miss out on some of your greatest experiences in life, only because your tribe deems it against their rules to interact with those outsiders. In some cases, you might even feel strong hate for those who are not part of your tribe. This hate is based on a fear of others being different. To prevent this, we need to stop assessing people based on their group, but rather individually. Not only will this decrease our fears, as we find more evidence that most people are safe to communicate with, but it will also open us to new opportunities to experience the world.

The divide between „us" and „them" can be very tempting because it makes us feel important. It creates the illusion of superiority. The others lack something that unites your group, whether it's power, skills, appearance, or beliefs. Many groups exhibit this behavior openly. However, some groups foster this divide subtly. It is not as obvious because they do not have any hate for those who are different from them. Instead, they have pity, giving them the same feeling of being superior.

In a sense, it is even more perverse, because the entire groups portray itself as a rescuer of another group. According to the drama triangle, this means that there must be a victim and a persecutor as well. They perceive a hierarchy, and instead of seeing them as brothers trying to survive and strive, they see them as incapable of fighting for themselves. Let us assume the less privileged group failed. It would be on their own account. But if they succeeded, it would be only because of the support, robbing them of their own achievements.

Someone with overprotective parents probably can relate to this. While the motivation of a parent would be fear, claimed to be love, in group settings, it is virtue signaling. There is a big difference between helping people whom you see as equals and helping people because you feel more privileged. One comes from love, and the other from a feeling of superiority or a feeling of guilt for being privileged. If it comes from love, you will want the other person to feel the success of changing their situation. If it comes from guilt or superiority, it does not matter to you how they have grown along the way.

Imagine you are a marathon runner, and you have a friend who wants to be more fit. Inspired by your success, they start running too. Would it help your friend if you carried them across the finish line? No. To truly help, you are cheering for them on the sidelines, bringing them water when they need it, and when they are asking you for advice, you try your best to teach them. If you had carried them along the entire way, not only would they become less fit, but it would also not be their achievement. But to question a generous king makes you the enemy of the people and the king.

Our journey is about finding inner peace before attempting to change the world. It is not up to us to fix the world. Leave the world in peace, and it will leave you in peace as well. But we can become aware of our own acting within it. There is no need to outwardly display virtues just to create a persona we know isn't truly us. Rather than trying to appear virtuous for others, we should strive to genuinely be virtuous for ourselves. This way, we can stand with dignity, knowing that our actions align with our words.

Now wasn't it a good thing that you are not religious? Don't worry, you are not unaffected by this play of human existence either. We all have relationships, and throughout a lifetime, it's nearly impossible not to fall into similar traps. These traps might involve family, a partner, friends, coworkers, or even your political affiliations.

Almost everyone has some level of engagement with politics, making it a great example. This book isn't about politics per se; it's about optimizing your life experiences. You might firmly believe that your political group holds the key to solving the world's crises. You may see the opposing group as the enemy, intent on destroying your country or even the world. Notice that I haven't specified your political affiliation, yet this statement holds true regardless of which side you're on. This means both sides believe they are acting for the greater good. Stalin, as well as Hitler, probably were convinced until the very end that they were on the side of the righteous. It sounds unthinkable, considering the number of atrocities they committed. But very likely it still is true. The hero of my story is me after all, no?

Consider the values and rules of your political group. Do you feel guilty about your actions? Do you find yourself angry at those who don't adhere to your group's beliefs? Do you feel like a victim of the opposing side? Whether you're deeply involved in politics or not, if you answer these questions honestly, it doesn't matter which group you align with. If the answer is often „yes," then you are stuck in a toxic relationship.

Probably, you will identify strongly as progressive or conservative. Even if your country provides other parties, you will identify with them. Your views on various issues likely match the ideology of your group, even if those issues aren't directly related. For example, opinions on national defense and education tend to align with group ideologies, despite being different fields. That seems to be an awfully convenient accident. Like religion, if someone questions even one aspect of your political group, they become a heretic. Again, you will find countless arguments as to why this is not true. Your ego might claim something like the problems in this world can only be fixed by your group, and the other side is either ignorant or straight-up lies about facts. But just like in religion, how can you be sure the other side is lying, and your side is correct?

In fact, any ideological group that endures the test of time will eventually become self-serving, if not outright malicious. A group without the ability to hold attention will simply fade away. To maintain attention over a long period, a clear goal is necessary, which is why ideological groups tend to outlast those lacking a strong guiding ideology. If a group's attention can be anchored to an unachievable goal, its survival is virtually guaranteed. For groups with achievable goals, however, the goalpost must be continually shifted to ensure their ongoing existence.

For the group's followers, achieving the original goal would present a fundamental threat to their sense of purpose. As a result, such groups rarely disband after achieving their aims. This phenomenon has been observed by anthropologists studying sects that predicted a specific date for doomsday. When the date came and went without the world ending, most members didn't abandon their beliefs in the face of contradictory evidence. Instead, they rationalized the situation, either shifting the date or assigning a new meaning to it. Rather than losing faith, they doubled down on their ideology. The fear of losing their sense of purpose and community outweighed the force of evidence.

In certain ideologies, once the original goal is overshot, an opposing group often emerges to claim attention. However, this „opposition" is merely the other side of the same pendulum, swinging to an extreme in the opposite direction. This shift usually doesn't occur because people wake up to the flaws in their ideology, but because the new generation gradually replaces the old.

14.5 Morals

Morals are agreements within groups to maintain order, and even animals follow unspoken rules that keep their packs or herds functioning. But when it comes to human morality, we often attach cosmic significance, particularly in religious contexts. It can feel strange to imagine a divine being micromanaging what people do in the bedroom or telling us how to behave in every detail of life. Penn Jillette captures this tension perfectly: „*I do rape all I want. And the amount I want is zero. And I do murder all I want, and the amount I want is zero. The fact that these people think that if they didn't have this person watching over them, they would go on killing and raping rampages is the most self-damning thing I can imagine. I don't want to do that. Right now, without any god, I don't want to jump across this table and strangle you. I have no desire to strangle you. I have no desire to flip you over and rape you.*"

In other words, if your moral compass truly depends on a supreme overseer peering into your thoughts, what does that say about your genuine intentions? Would you lose all civility the moment you stopped believing you were under surveillance? For most people, the answer is no; they simply don't want to harm others. Yet, when groups or institutions insist that only their rules stand between us and chaotic evil, they're undercutting our innate capacity for empathy and cooperation.

The truth is **moral behavior is any action that increases overall well-being**. That's it. The details get messy because different communities measure „*well-being*" in wildly different ways, and many people fear that giving

215

certain groups more freedom will threaten their traditions or personal beliefs.

Take, for example, a religious fanatic who might be disturbed by gay marriage. They're temporarily uncomfortable, yes, but if the arrangement significantly improves the quality of life for countless same-sex couples, wouldn't it be morally justifiable on balance? By that same indicator, some practices deemed *moral* by a particular group (e.g., discriminating against or shaming others) can degrade well-being and thus become immoral. Using this indicator, we can see that some so-called moral actions are actually immoral. The challenge is how to measure well-being.

Measuring well-being is indeed tricky. Emotions, subjective preferences, and cultural biases all come into play. Yet some societies have tried creative approaches, like **Bhutan's Gross National Happiness Index**, which treats happiness as a genuine benchmark of a nation's success. Whether or not that system is perfect, it does point to a broader question: how do we design societal *rules* that improve people's lives instead of just controlling them?

The conflict between freedom and safety is not merely a political or social dilemma. It is a moral one. Under the guise of *safety*, fear is often weaponized to manipulate people into surrendering their liberties, trading autonomy for a fleeting sense of security. Such decisions carry profound ethical consequences, as they risk undermining the moral agency that allows individuals to make meaningful choices. As Benjamin Franklin warned, „*Those who would give up essential liberty to purchase a little temporary safety deserve neither liberty nor safety."* By clinging to safety at any cost, we empower those who seek control, sacrificing the moral imperative to uphold dignity, individuality, and creativity. Truly moral actions prioritize the freedom to think and act responsibly, fostering genuine flourishing over the hollow illusion of guaranteed security.

Ultimately, morality has always been about equilibrium: striking a balance between personal freedom and the collective good. The next time someone claims there's only one correct moral stance, be it from a pulpit or a political stage, remember that morals aren't just edicts from on high. They're agreements we form to navigate life together, ideally in ways that cause less harm and create more genuine happiness for everyone involved.

14.6 Deprogramming

Yuval Harari emphasizes an unsettling reality about this century: „I think the most important thing for people to realize about living in the 21st century, as against the Middle Ages or the Stone Age, is that we are now hackable animals." In other words, entire groups, whether political parties or global movements, can steer our views without us realizing it, locking us into divisive 'us vs. them' echo chambers. This suggests that our political beliefs might not truly be our own. If Louis XVI had access to today's data-crunching, machine learning, and psychological tools, the French Revolution might never have occurred. Social media has amplified this influence, creating echo chambers that manipulate opinions and emotions on a massive scale. The age-old strategy of

„divide and conquer" remains effective in the modern era, yet many remain oblivious to how deeply they are entangled in this manipulative game, often sacrificing their peace for programmed goals.

For those ensnared by ideologies, interactions are no longer about genuinely meeting another human being. It is about categorizing the other person and finding what unites or divides us. This mindset traps us in an echo chamber, where we demonize people who might otherwise be good-natured. We mistake the roles of rescuer or victim in the drama triangle for virtues and, in doing so, compel others to fit into these roles as well. We indulge in the drama, ultimately dehumanizing those we perceive as persecutors. You might think your group is immune to·these dynamics, but that's just a comforting lie our egos tell us. This entrapment in group roles often leads to actions that ripple far beyond our intentions, as history shows.

When Alan Watts said the following: „Furthermore, as muddy water is best cleared by leaving it alone, it could be argued that those who sit quietly and do nothing are making one of the best possible contributions to a world in turmoil." He highlighted the idea that do-gooders often have the best intentions, yet their actions can inadvertently swing the pendulum to the other side. This principle can be seen in recent events, such as the shooting of Donald Trump. The shooter, in an attempt to influence the political landscape, inadvertently was a factor in securing Trump's election victory. It was clear to many that this would be the consequence, yet the strong convictions of individuals often blind them to the broader impact of their actions.

If people could detach from the intense emotions of the political game and engage in meaningful dialogue with those who think differently, they could reach evidence-based conclusions together. Given the growing challenges, it is essential to understand that we need the „*others*" to pull the wagon out of the mud. However, in our current political climate, any questioning of either group's stance is seen as an attack, creating a toxic interdependence. This makes it difficult to cultivate healthier relationships, as described by David Emerald's roles of creator, challenger, and coach, rather than victim, persecutor, and rescuer. If you are discussing with your loved one, you don't throw a vase. Instead, you take a step back, let the water clear, and have a conversation when both are calm.

To maintain clarity of mind and avoid falling into the savior or victim roles, it is beneficial to become an observer. This allows for participation in the political game with greater awareness and a balanced perspective, fostering more constructive and less reactive interactions. Besides, not everything and everyone needs to be political. You don't impose your political ideologies on a flower. Politics is a game of power, and some are simply not interested in playing it. It can be a hindrance on one's spiritual journey.

When you take the position of the observer, you will find that it was never complicated to break free from the ideological clutches. If you can't see the path yet, it might reveal itself in these pages. Sadly, we will only understand how bad something is for us when we go through that experience once. The suffering of being stuck in a toxic relationship becomes the reference experience for the future. If we refuse the lessons that we were supposed to learn, then a similar situation will arise again.

I'm not suggesting you become a hermit, though it might sound tempting at times. We need social interaction. Studies show that not being part of a tribe negatively affects our health. It gives us comfort and a feeling of being loved. Your best relationships are the ones where you feel genuinely appreciated. However, it's essential to choose relationships based not on our flawed understanding of love but on a clearer perspective, free from past traumas and misconceptions. You want the groups you are participating in to enrich your life. This also means that you must similarly participate in the group, or the dynamic might be disturbed. Engage only in groups where you can actively contribute and add value.

Groups are almost like energetic beings; they feed off your attention. By not giving them any, they will stop engaging. True detachment can even break group patterns by changing the frame of interaction, which means that if you can conjure up the wrath of a group, there is a simple solution to resolve this. You genuinely must not care. Pretending not to care will not do the trick. Only if you can be relaxed while this rottweiler clenches their jaws into you, then you have a chance that it will let go. If you are without guilt and can admit to the evidence unequivocally, then there is nothing to latch onto. Given, of course, that the evidence suggests that you acted in the best interest. But if you feel guilty or angry, even if it is unrighteous, then you can expect a muddy fight.

14.7 Framing

A frame is a mental structure that shapes how information is perceived and interpreted. When two people hold different beliefs about an outcome, each carries an expectation that forms their premise. If you firmly hold your belief, others might eventually adjust theirs, assuming that your frame was more correct, unless there is strong evidence suggesting otherwise.

Groups will also shift their goals if you maintain your belief with unwavering conviction, particularly when their entire modus operandi rests on weak evidence. Angry mobs, for instance, frequently run on raw emotion over facts, making them prone to adopt whatever seems most convincing in the heat of the moment. However, if you submit to the group's belief, even with weak evidence, it becomes reality. The more people believe a certain outcome, the more likely it becomes. Which means great actors make skillful politicians. Not that we need such.

When I visited my friend Farid in Tulum, we made use of that. Prices for parties in Tulum are ridiculously high, and I refused to pay them. My friend was not worried at all. We went out, and as usual, he knew people that we met at the club entrance who had a table. He assumed immediately that he would be invited to join. He assumed we'd be invited to join, while I felt it would be overbearing. Both of our frames became a reality, and they said they could take one more person. My friend, being the trickster he is, wasn't worried about this at all. He told me to give him my top and meet him from the beach side, which was not the official entrance. So, I went topless to the bouncer at the beach entrance, who obviously was confused about where I was coming from. But before he could tell me to leave, my friend came along with my shirt. Being in on the heist, I believed this time that I was going to be able to join the club. The bouncer was faced with two belief systems confronting his own. One of them was my friend's unshakable conviction that we would have a great evening in this club. He eventually faltered and let me in. Leading to an unforgettable evening.

This, of course, is a play with fire, as the other person might have a stronger conviction than you. Standing before the bouncer, I genuinely didn't care whether I got in or not. I knew I'd enjoy the night with my friend regardless. I was not scared of the consequences either. But if you are fine with any outcome and, therefore, are unattached, then usually, social dynamics will shift in your favor. But to do so, you must be able to let go of the outcome.

This is the closest to a Jedi mind trick we will come to. But be aware that if you bend reality too much, it will backfire. You will create wrong expectations, or the other person is fully aware of what you are doing. We all have a subconscious social credit score over our heads, and while it might seem that you gained benefits initially, people will not forget. If even the trickster god Loki couldn't dodge punishment for his mischief, what makes you think you'll avoid judgment entirely?

When framing is weaponized to make others doubt their own reality, we call it gaslighting. Every interaction unfolds within some kind of frame, and those with dubious motives often excel at shaping it. While genuine conviction usually grows from actual competence, some people learn to *fake* competence by exuding sheer confidence, an instinctive survival strategy. This makes them appear very confident in their beliefs. In relationships, we interact not only with individuals but also with groups. While individuals face consequences for their actions, groups often do not. It is crucial to recognize the influence that environments have on us. Both individuals and groups with malicious intent share similar traits: grandiosity, an unwavering belief that they are always right, an inflated sense of self-importance, a lack of empathy, a tendency to blame others, difficulty adjusting to change, exploitive behavior, and strong reactions when their beliefs are challenged.

If you use it not to manipulate reality but, for example, to make a heavy situation lighthearted and fun by making a joke, then there are no repercussions. Suppose you can engage with enthusiasm and compassion in a challenging conversation instead of being scared. It does not disturb any balances, and therefore, there is no punishment to be expected. While my first friend is a bit of a trickster, my friend Anna is a master of *positive reframing*. She engages everyone with extraordinary compassion and lightheartedness. If people feel like you care for them, then they will reciprocate this feeling.

We were on a trip through Portugal and rented a car. All of us had a bad night of sleep, and our attention was really exhausted. So, no one realized that we had just turned into a road that was not meant for cars. The road became so narrow that we could not go on. Not only was the road very narrow, but it was also very steep, and on one side, it would drop us into some family's house. We were essentially stuck. With great effort, we managed to turn the car, but did not avoid damaging the car in the process. We even got help from a local. Even though the car was saved, it was not in good condition. While we had insurance, the prospect of dealing with an angry car rental was nothing to look forward to. The car was rented under Anna's name, which meant she had to return it. Anna returned the car with such compassion that the rental employee didn't even mention the damage. Her frame set a tone of understanding, making the situation stress-free for both. If she had handled the situation any differently, it would probably have been a stressful experience. For her, compassion comes naturally, but it is something that can be practiced.

14.8 Choosing the Right Communities

Knowing that we will always adjust to the groups around us sounds like a dooming judgment. But this is not true at all. It means that we can take control of who we become by changing the people, groups, and influences around us. The easiest way to exclude negative influences is by not having them physically around you. In the information age, this includes social media. If you limit your device to purposeful use, rather than mindless entertainment, you'll reduce how often digital groups and social media hijack your attention.

The people you invest most of your attention in should reflect the state of awareness you're cultivating because we inevitably absorb traits and mindsets from our closest circles. At the same time, actively seeking out and nurturing groups that uplift and inspire you is just as important. Communities have the power to magnify your strengths, challenge you to grow, and provide support during difficult times. A strong group fosters a sense of belonging and mutual growth, encouraging each member to reach their potential while offering a safe space to be authentic. Research has shown that positive social connections can reduce stress, boost mental health, and even improve physical well-being by strengthening the immune system. Surrounding yourself with such groups not only accelerates personal development but also adds richness and depth to your life. The right group doesn't just shape who you are. They help you envision and strive for who you could become.

We all have shortcomings, but if someone displays attributes you don't want in your life, you'll need to constantly resist adopting them. If they are a great disturbance, you might need to cut ties. But always consider if you have higher standards for your friends than yourself. Always be stricter with yourself before making harsh decisions. You can change your path, not others. Imagine an untimely scoundrel being disappointed in you for being late. It means they value their time but not yours. Marcus Aurelius gave the following advice to avoid becoming a scoundrel yourself: „Be *tolerant with others and strict with yourself.*"

If you feel stuck, maybe it's time to throw yourself into new waters. Change cities and build a new personality. Every new place I moved to changed my personality. In going through this process, I realized that the groups, people, and even the thoughts I identified with weren't actually 'me.' They were layers I'd taken on rather than reflections of my true nature. The world is changing anyway, so why not increase the pace and push your comfort zone? Talk to strangers, attend new events, and start solo traveling.

My journey led me to become a nomad, constantly in new environments. This either forced me to interact with others to make friends or be comfortable alone. Both states are good teachers. Be conscious of your comfort zone's limits. The process should be fun. Know when you've over-challenged yourself and when the challenge wasn't enough. Once you embrace this mindset, life becomes a playful arena brimming with challenges that sharpen your growth. True freedom often resides just beyond the boundaries of your comfort zone.

Don't be discouraged from finding good relationships; they are more important than material goods. Imagine being wealthy but with no real friends. It would be a sad existence. A strong social circle helps in hard times. Fooling around with friends can be more helpful than anything else. It decreases the situation's importance, making it easier to enjoy.

So, how do we know if a relationship is a good one? The person or group will have no strong social hierarchies; they won't victimize you and won't deem outsiders as inferior. Such groups will give off a feeling of ease, not forcing anything onto you or others, and it is easy to dip in and out.

Don't judge others based on their social hierarchies because you will miss out on a lot of experiences. Hierarchy can only exist by comparing based on arbitrary standards, which only makes sense in a group setting. A group that is nurturing our well-being is usually a group that has a lot of individuals not acting based on hierarchies.

As ironic as it may seem, while writing this, I was sitting in a coffee shop, overhearing a conversation between two people complaining. One proudly proclaimed, at some point, that a third person, being part of the same group, had just recently found her activism, which, therefore, her opinion was worth less. This was awfully ironic and yet entertaining for me. But it seems the hierarchical rules suppressed the freedom of their adherents, making the entire endeavor of freeing some suppressed group of people rather questionable, doesn't it?

If you judge yourself based on hierarchies, you're forced into perpetual comparison, making it impossible to simply be yourself. A mythical figure like the Buddha or Jesus would probably not judge at all, but as humans, we do. Judging is a mechanism to find out if a person is a threat or a friend. Therefore, if there is a need to judge individuals, not their groups or standing within them, reduce your judgment to the bare minimum and only consider if a person has a frequency that you enjoy swinging with or not.

15 Attention
The Currency of Life

Attention is a valuable currency. If you don't know how to spend it wisely, you won't gain anything in return. We also crave the attention of others. Attention is what creates value in this world. Consider this: if you're attentive to crops, they will grow and nourish you. If you focus on your work, you'll create something valuable. If you nurture your relationships, they will be long-lasting. When others give us their attention, we often perceive it as love. To harness this valuable attention, we must first understand how it is shaped by awareness.

Any group can only thrive if its members invest attention in it. When something or someone captures your attention, it can spark a desire within you, forming the foundation of marketing and social media. The work we do is also a profound form of attention. By dedicating time and effort to our tasks, we infuse our labor with value. Attention can then be transformed into currency when people pay for it. In essence, natural resources and human attention are the primary reasons currencies exist. Currencies themselves hold no inherent value; they function solely as a medium for exchanging and storing value. Throughout history, many currencies, like the Song dynasty Jiaozi, have disappeared and been replaced when people lost faith in them and sought new methods of exchange. Despite this, we are conditioned to prioritize money over attention, even though it is attention that truly holds value.

15.1 Dancing with Intention

Awareness is the foundation of attention. When we focus awareness, it transforms into attention, allowing us to concentrate deliberately on what truly matters. This state of deep engagement is what gives us the power to shape our experiences and align with the present moment. Attention sharpens our perception and connects us to the here and now, creating clarity and purpose. In these moments of deep focus, the ego momentarily disappears, allowing you to experience life without the endless commentary of your own mind. This clarity is both powerful and liberating, reminding us that behind our thoughts and worries, there is a calm center that simply observes. This calm center of observation becomes the foundation for directing our attention with purpose.

To direct our attention effectively, we need intent. Intention is the commitment to act, distinguishing it from mere desire. When you put attention where your intention is, you will find that the world will fall into place. The difference between someone who can focus their attention for only a short time and someone who can focus their attention for a long time is resilience. The eternal „*now*" is guided by our attention or, in Epictetus's words, „*You become what you give your attention to.*"

Human attention is a precious resource, and others will desire your attention, be it the news, social media, objects, work, friends, or family. The better you become at directing your attention, the more value it has to others. Someone who can devote significant attention to something will be able to accomplish harder things. Mathematicians, for instance, are well-compensated because they can solve problems that others cannot. If you can do things no one else can do, it makes you rare. It's your choice whether or not you join that competition. But once you do, others will judge your value in that field. However, the value others assign to your attention can influence how you perceive yourself, if you let it.

It is very important to point out that you leave it to others to judge. It is not up to you what others think. Burdening yourself with their judgment is detrimental. You will allow others to not only judge your value on the market but also your value towards yourself as well. The games we are involved in have different ways of judging the value of the players. The same person will be judged differently in

231

a different environment. If we, therefore, give ourselves a value based on these arbitrary games, then our value will always be shifting. It will be based on the groups we are in. If we decide that these arbitrary values these groups dictate have no bearing on us, then we are finally free from this restriction. Instead of comparing ourselves to others, we want to engage in these games for the joy of playing them.

A friend once complained about bodybuilders and celebrities setting unattainable beauty and fitness standards, making life harder for others. Unaware that he was still caught in the game of duality. When you truly let go of your judgment, you will not be bothered by them being good at the game. Instead, you will be inspired by what humans are capable of achieving without comparing yourself to them, as that would create a rift between you and them again. Your journey is unique, even if it resembles theirs. Yet, not everyone sees the world through this lens of personal freedom, as societal pressures often frame life as a competition.

Some people are blind to human nature and claim there is no competition. For some, this ignorance is bliss, as the mindset to compete can be unhealthy. If you compete with everyone about everything, you inevitably suffer. Notice which competitions you feel drawn to participate in. Now, ask yourself if you define yourself based on that competition. For example, you might feel ugly, but only because you identify with beauty standards. You might feel untalented, but only because you compare yourself to talented people. You signal to your mind that you are not enough and need to be more. Despite this predicament, we need to engage with society, and within society, there is much competition.

The problem is not the competitions themselves; they make society better and push you to generate more value for yourself and others. The issue lies in our internal judgment of these situations. Self-worth is an illusion. We estimate our worth within a certain system and create internal hierarchies between ourselves and others. While we should be mindful of which competitions we choose to enter, we should also be aware of how they influence our internal world. If we must compete, we should treat it like a game. Whether we win or lose doesn't matter. We are never the judge of the outcome of our work. We create, but we leave it to others to judge the results. Ironically, by being independent of the outcome, we become better creators, partners, artists, or businesspeople.

Be mindful of where you place your attention. Focusing on unattainable things or things you cannot change is wasted energy. Modern marketing exploits this by constantly shifting our attention to things we supposedly need. To sell something, it is necessary to create dissatisfaction. This creates a perpetual desire for unattainable things. The same goes for politics; if you lack the power to influence political outcomes but are emotionally invested, you'll have no attention left for your well-being, leaving you feeling stuck or, even worse, a victim. One option is to become politically active and gain some degree of control. People who are active in their communities show higher degrees of happiness. Ideally, we should aim not to overly identify with these external factors.

But once we shift attention to the things that we have control over, we can start navigating. Ask yourself if your actions can change a situation. If not, you're wasting your attention.

We often make decisions based on fear, be it fear of failure, rejection, or missing out. But there's another compass worth following: your excitement. Excitement is a quiet whisper from your authentic self, guiding you toward alignment. When you follow what genuinely excites you, you no longer need to force motivation; your energy regenerates naturally. Fear might get you moving, but only excitement can sustain the journey. Shifting from fear-based action to inspiration-based living frees you from survival mode and places you into a state of flow. Let your attention be pulled by curiosity and aliveness, not dragged by anxiety and expectation.

By concentrating on what we can change, we gradually progress, sometimes gaining momentum, allowing us to ride a wave of good fortune. As Seneca wisely said, „*He who has control over himself has control over the world.*"

15.2 Freed from Distraction

We first need to find out what we want to do with our attention because otherwise, we will not stick to the process. Once we become untangled from the groups, it will become easier to see our own goals as well. It quiets the voices within us that disguise themselves as our own. Your goals could be your childhood dreams before parents and schools left an imprint. You might discover your true passions by trying different things. Ask yourself questions and observe your feelings. Do you enjoy working with people? Creating art? Building something valuable? Distributing products? Are you looking for a partner? Do you love learning or teaching? Find the questions that spark excitement within you. As you explore these questions, it's crucial to distinguish your true desires from the influences around you.

Be cautious not to confuse your answers with others' expectations. A positive emotional response might come from making others happy, but it's not your responsibility to fulfill their happiness.

To achieve our goals, we must focus our attention on them. However, our ego often exaggerates their importance. From a young age, we are taught that goals are crucial, leading to inner resistance rather than motivation for many children. The heavier the perceived importance, the worse they perform. Parents and teachers often mislabel struggling children as troublemakers or dumb, not realizing that reducing the weight of expectations can help.

Good parents teach their children to enjoy the journey, not just the outcome. Studies show that external validation, like rewards, diminishes intrinsic motivation. Children should learn to find joy in the process itself. Giving rewards teaches children that they are in it for the outcome and not for the journey. These lessons from childhood carry into adulthood, where our focus on outcomes can hinder our progress.

Dependence on the outcome will stifle our abilities and create resistance within us. Sure, we can fight things for a while, but eventually, this will make us sick, exhausted, or depressed. Many of us learned this pattern from an early age, and we will continue applying this later in life. After all, we do not like to work for free, and we will preserve energy if we have a choice. But a person playing a game without the need for an outcome in their mind will not stop playing the game. Meanwhile, the person having an outcome in mind will stop once the outcome is reached or when the amount of energy needed is exhausted. But the person who is outcome independent will not deplete their energy. To the contrary, the process will even energize them. The person focused on an outcome sees fierce competition, while the one playing an endless game simply enjoys the process. What matters is surviving to play another round.

Who will be the better runner: the one aiming to run a marathon in a certain time or the one who loves running?

The popular belief is that if you work exceptionally hard, you will be successful. But while I worked hard to write this book, I cannot expect it to be successful. You can create the best conditions for a plant to grow, making it more likely that it will grow, yet it might die, and another plant with worse conditions might flourish. All we can do is create the circumstances, and we create them by enjoying the path. This book was not created with an expectation. But I hope exactly this is what makes it a good read. I enjoyed my time learning and writing about these things. Therefore, it is already a success. If it turns out to be a wasted effort, then so be it. But I had a great time doing so.

A good example of outcome independence is dating. Imagine yourself approaching an attractive person of the opposite gender; if you are honest, you will find that it induces fear. It is a natural reaction, as it means you are introducing a risk into your life. After all, the person might be dangerous, and the fear runs even deeper, as our tribalistic mind suggests, that their tribe might consider us a threat. But we all know people who seem to have no fear of this. The difference lies in the framing within their mind. They created evidence, often with great effort, that in modern times, there is almost no risk involved.

Most will never come to this conclusion and, therefore, would never dare to talk to someone they find attractive. The most common path to push through this fear is to numb it with alcohol or other drugs. Another way would be to deal with your fears. Besides evidence that your ancestral fears are unwarranted, becoming outcome-independent would lift your fear of rejection. Now imagine these three people: one would probably stand in the corner not doing anything, the other would be drunk, awkward, or both, and the third would at least try to have a conversation. This third person, unattached to validation from others, will be authentic and, in their own way, charming. Of course, this does not mean everyone will treat them kindly and love them, but it does not bother them. Just as we cannot even agree on what makes good food, not everyone will agree on what makes a good partner. Not being outcome-dependent will not spoil the game either, as they can just walk away if a person reacts bitterly.

This principle is vital not just for first meetings but also in relationships. When we start projecting expectations onto a relationship, we sabotage it. If both partners are outcome-independent, they can enjoy each other's company without needing to change one another. They can accept the quirks of someone else without forcing them to change. After all, as an independent person, you do not need anything from the other person. But hopefully, they will add to the scenery on your path. In the best case, they might even support you on your journey, but expecting it will spoil the relationship. This independence in relationships mirrors the broader truth that personal transformation begins within.

No one other than you can change your life. If you want to increase your physical abilities, for example, a trainer can guide you, but they can't do the exercises for you. The same applies to all areas of life. Happiness can't come from demanding that society change; it must come from your own actions. Complaining and envy indicate a lack of control over one's life. Those who focus on external circumstances instead of internal changes will blame the outside world for their problems, never asking what they could have done better. This mindset dooms them to repeat the same negative experiences until they become bitter. As we are human, we must allow ourselves to release our frustration. But there is a difference between allowing the emotion to flow through us once and repeating it again and again. The situation will not change. By holding on to it, you repeat the suffering every time you bring it back into your awareness. The process of letting go once more becomes important here.

Complainers will perceive reality as something bad. Our perception of reality is our truth of reality. We focus our attention on the bad things; therefore, we do not have space for the good things. Shifting attention to things to be grateful for will change this reality. Those aware of this will be careful not to waste energy by perpetually needing to shift their perspective to a positive one. They avoid this bittersweet trap of indulging in the hormonal cocktail that our shared suffering brings. Once it becomes addictive, it will be hard to change the pattern. However, it means that you are trapped in permanent suffering as you are going through your experience repeatedly. Instead of learning from it, your pain becomes stronger and stronger. To maintain inner peace, your only option is to walk away from complaining and complainers. If you are not walking away, you will have to put a lot of attention into not being affected, wasting valuable resources.

How we distribute our attention is influenced by the people we spend time with and how engaging our tasks are. Mundane or overly challenging tasks can make us either want to alter the challenge or change our perception of it. Many are either not aware of how challenged they are, or they don't ask the environment to adjust. It is crucial to stay engaged in our work, though. If you hate working out or wealthy people, you probably won't enjoy fitness or financial success. Negative associations prevent us from learning and growing in these areas.

Such negative associations usually come from an internal hierarchy that forms when we do not do well in this area of life. To mask this inadequacy, we flip the hierarchy. Now, a very fit or rich person is perceived as someone who is damaged. To succeed, we must drop the hierarchy and approach life with love for the things we want to nurture. Loving something doesn't mean being attached

239

to it, as Rabbi Abraham Twerski's „*fish-love*" illustrates. By loving the challenges of life, we love ourselves.

By starting to love the games of life, you will start to love yourself. Love does not mean you indulge in the things that will give you a temporary dopamine hit. If you love your dog, you will not feed the dog chocolate. You will look for dog food that has the most nutritional value. But when it comes to us, we will just indulge in things that are harmful to ourselves. Some will even claim that eating cake or drinking alcohol is self-love. They are fully aware of the negative long-term effects of their endeavors. The problem is our inner framing of what is going on.

While groups indeed have their influence on it as well, some of it is biological. High-caloric foods were rare in the past, and this means we don't need to worry for a while about finding more food. The dopamine spike was just the body's way of rewarding us for finding once-rare resources. However, as life becomes easier, we have an excess of resources. Today's abundance requires us to regulate our dopamine spikes. Like Pavlov's dogs, we need to condition ourselves to healthy behaviors. Excessive indulgence in screens, smoking, drinking, or partying will dull the satisfaction from real achievements. Celebrating occasionally is fine, but frequent indulgence diminishes the joy of genuine success.

Being mindful of how we spend our time and letting go of activities that do not bring us closer to living the life that we want is crucial. The way you live your moments will decide what your days will become, your days decide how you will look at this year, and your years will influence how you live your life. Every moment, you decide anew what kind of life you want to live. It is not about the great changes we make in life, but all about the small habits. I used to play a lot of video games, which was holding me back from my vision of life. Become aware of the intent that arises when you are about to direct your attention to something. If you feel that your intent is not toward your goal, ask yourself if you are doing it to distract yourself or to have a celebration of life. If it is a distraction, you might want to feel the emotions arising. Let it flow through you instead of resisting it, and take immediate action toward your purpose. This will generate abundance and freedom in your life instead of falling into addictive patterns.

15.3 The Brain Game

It seems these days that everyone suffers from ADHD. It is often used as an excuse to shirk responsibilities. The easy solution to this conundrum seems to be to medicate everybody. Instead of curing the cause, we are treating the symptoms. We do this by giving people drugs that basically flood the brain with dopamine. The right way, however, would be to only stimulate the part of our brain responsible for resilience and attention, which is called the anterior midcingulate cortex. Imagine if there were a part in an engine not working properly. Would you flood the entire engine with oil? It would be a foolish way of fixing it. This way, loads of new problems are generated.

Neuroplasticity research shows that we can reshape our brains even in adulthood. Doing hard things daily helps train this part of the brain. Working out, meditating in challenging conditions, or starting with small, manageable tasks can build resilience. Forming habits starts with consistently showing up, and over time, this builds capacity and strength. If we make it a habit to do something hard every day, then, of course, our brain is going to adapt to this new behavior. A particularly effective habit: work out every day. This will put the wheels in motion for that part of the brain to develop, besides having many more benefits for your body. But maybe you feel like meditating under a freezing river like a monk. Of course, if you have that one thing that you really want to do, then start doing the thing and later add more challenging tasks. To illustrate how small, consistent efforts can build this resilience, consider a moment from my own life.

It was during lunch at university when a good friend hit a serious low point. She'd just found out she flunked her exams and was having a full-blown meltdown. Through sniffles and tears, she asked me how I managed to deal with my own slow crawl toward finishing university. Her voice was shaky, her frustration palpable. I took a moment, then hit her with something totally unexpected: „*How do you eat an elephant?*" She stopped crying mid-sob, looking at me like I'd completely lost it. „*What?*" she asked, bewildered. I grinned and replied, „*One bite at a time.*" The absurdity of the image made her giggle, and that tiny laugh was the breakthrough she needed.

The idea clicked for both of us: even the biggest mess can be tackled if you just take it one step at a time. Start with small things, and don't try to overreach your capacities.

You can't just learn a handstand. You start by practicing on the wall. For any habit we want to form, the most crucial part is showing up. Let's assume you want to become fit. Your focus shouldn't be to lift heavy weights right away, but simply to go to the gym regularly. Since you're there anyway, you might as well do some exercises, regardless of the volume. Over time, those small steps add up, and before you know it, the elephant doesn't seem so big anymore.

It is only about the path, not about competing. Sometimes, we make significant strides, and other times, we take only small steps. There is, however, a daunting realization that comes with this, as this means that comfort is not a thing that you are striving for anymore. It means you make discomfort your friend without overexerting yourself. Only by putting yourself in uncomfortable positions can you become comfortable in them. Like easing into a difficult yoga pose, we learn to relax in discomfort, enhancing our adaptability and making us more flexible in life as well.

Increasing your resilience enhances your available attention. We can achieve this by exercising our anterior prefrontal cortex through challenging tasks or meditation. However, our mind has less influence on resilience than we might believe; our physical state determines how much energy we have in the face of adversity. Dopamine, testosterone, and cortisol play a more significant role than anything else. Refer to the chapter about the body if needed.

Awareness and attention shape our reality. By directing our focus and letting go of unhelpful patterns, we create positive changes. Life's journey is more like navigating a speedboat in a wild river than driving a slow-moving car. Life is happening too fast for your mind to calculate. If you listen to your heart, however, you might be able to navigate in the middle of a raging storm.

Through it all, remember the tremendous power in moments of focused attention. These are the times you are purely aware of what is before you. In such moments, the constant voice of the ego temporarily quiets, gifting you a direct experience of whatever is happening. This unfiltered connection with the present is both the essence of awareness and the foundation of truly living your life from your own center.

The poodle's core

"That I understand what holds the core of the world together, and this is exactly the gist of the matter."— Goethe.

In the original German text, „the gist of the matter" translates to „the poodle's core." Throughout history, the search for the meaning of life has preoccupied humanity's greatest minds. Yet, the answers seem elusive. Religions, science, and spiritual Leaders try to find this meaning, but without much success. If we look externally, we might never find an answer to it, as we are system imminent. But maybe the place we are looking at is the wrong place, maybe the answers are found internally. This inward search for meaning became a personal quest, one I explored through simple yet profound questions in my youth.

In my early college years, I loved to ask the question, „Who are you?" to start an interaction. It's surprising how often people are either baffled or simply answer with their names. I rarely pressed further, though their responses often felt unsatisfying. Despite its simplicity, „Who are you?" is far from an easy question to answer, and I suspect most people struggle with it. Most would answer with their name, but that is barely two words given to you by your parents. As many will not have a real answer to it, they will define themselves by external sources.

What a travesty it would be for a consumerist society if people had other ways of defining themselves other than the things they buy. We try to express who we are with our clothes and how our rooms look, don't we? This works for the outside world, but inside, we know that it is not us either. Some will define themselves based on their skills; they are surfers, skiers, or good worker bees. Others will define themselves with their ideologies and the corresponding groups they are in; they are German, American, Christian, Muslim, Communist, Capitalist, etc. But at this point, we know that this would only describe an aspect of the ego. Maybe Taylor Durden in Fight Club was right: „You are not your job, you're not how much money you have in the bank. You are not the car you drive. You're not the contents of your wallet. You are not your fucking khakis. You are all singing, all dancing crap of the world." Yet, beneath these false identities lies a deeper truth, accessible only when we quiet the external noise.

The issue lies in the fact that you are not listening to what the universe whispers. Your ears are blocked by all these definitions of yourself. Knowing who you are is nothing to be defined; it is something to be experienced. Once what separates us from the world becomes quiet, we start to fall into the endless cycles of existence. I would lie if I said that I did not know the experience, as deep meditation is very similar to what a psychedelic experience is to me. But instead of forcing open the door with a substance, we aim to achieve it naturally. And in a way, life itself is a psychedelic experience. You just don't realize it most of the time. The constant unfolding of reality, the way moments bleed into each other, the impermanence of every sensation, thought, and feeling— it's all there, but the mind clings to its identifications, dulling the experience. Only when these layers loosen do we begin to glimpse what has always been right in front of us. This glimpse of unfiltered reality mirrors the profound shifts some encounter in altered states of consciousness.

Any experienced psychonaut will know the initial feeling of chaos that ensues before the journey truly begins. The very thing that separates you from the rest of the world is fighting for its survival, showing you all kinds of pictures and repeating all kinds of mantras that define it. But in the end, it has no choice but to die. Ego death, what a scary image for many, and probably rightfully so, as not everybody is prepared to wrestle with their very existence. No need to worry, as it will rise like Jesus from its grave after the journey has ended. The fear, however, is precedented, as there is no future or past in the state, and as such, one could say it vanishes forever. How could it travel with us while we are realizing that we are the entire universe, and the universe is us. Or, as Jim Carrey put it, „I used to be a guy who was experiencing the Universe, but now I feel like the Universe experiencing a guy."

Our usual copilot in this experience has meaning within the regular understanding of reality, but once the borders between everything dissolve, it becomes a hindrance. After all, the ego is exactly what constitutes this dichotomy. Without it, the entire play would not make sense, as we would not be separate characters with our separate challenges and desires, making it a boring endeavor altogether. The ego distributes meaning to our temporary existence. It is what is needed to create friction with the world. In moments when the ego's friction dissolves, we experience a flow that redefines our connection to existence.

The psychedelic journey is best represented as a state of frictionless flow between moments. Imagine all existence being compressed into one point, every moment happening at the same time, and you just flow through them without holding onto them. Time has no meaning here, as we are traveling through moments, regardless of their chronological occurrence. I am quoting myself here: „It feels as if you are a bouncy ball, which compressed all existence into this very moment, and then someone throws the ball into the infinite. Eventually bouncing back into this very moment." But the truth is, you don't need substances to access this state. It is always available. The more you let go of identifications, the more frequently these moments arise naturally. This is why we have spent so much time in this book dismantling identification with body, time, and environment so that these glimpses of

Satori stop being rare, fleeting events and instead become an ongoing unfolding of existence.

Before Siddhartha reached his divinity, he was faced with Mara, a symbolic demon that represents the *force of desire*. A great tempter holding us back from our divine nature. This symbolic force uses trickery to prevent you from seeing through the veil. Mara's tools to disconnect you from the divine are fear, doubt, and glamour.

A concept yet not much addressed in this book is glamour. It is so deeply woven into the fabric of our society and into our own self-image that most don't even notice it. Its shimmering promise wraps itself around us like a spell. Glamour is the desire for beauty, wealth, and external validation, dressed up as empowerment. But behind its sparkle lies a hidden hunger: the desire for control. Control over how we are perceived. Control over outcomes. Control over the world.

Glamour whispers that if we can perfect the image, if we are rich enough, beautiful enough, impressive enough, we will finally be worthy. But this is a lie. It is the ego's attempt to imitate the divine. Yet because it comes from a sense of lack, it can never reach it. You can become the wealthiest man or the most beautiful woman, and still feel hollow, because the pursuit comes from disconnection. You are not embodying the divine; you are compensating for the absence of it.

Even in the spiritual community, Mara adapts. It wears a robe and speaks in affirmations. It sells manifestation as another tool to get control over the physical world. „Manifest your dream life, your soulmate, your millions." But this, too, is Mara's glamour. The ego cloaked in spiritual language, trying to command the universe to obey its will. It assumes that the universe is something *other*, something to manipulate, rather than something we are meant to dance with in surrender.

We rarely ask who is doing the manifesting. Is it your awareness or your ego? The ego is not a reliable guide for your soul's unfolding. It doesn't know what you truly need. It only knows patterns, borrowed desires from childhood, from trauma, from society, and the media. It sets goals rooted in comparison, insecurity, and fear. And when you manifest from that place, you are not stepping into alignment. You are simply asking the universe to reinforce your illusions (Maya), to decorate your prison cell, rather than free you from it.

Surprisingly, one of my earliest meditations sparked what many traditions describe as a Kundalini awakening. I had no expectations, no prior knowledge of the term, just a quiet moment of tuning in. Suddenly, a wave of energy rose from the base of my spine and burst upward through my body, flooding me with an inexplicable bliss. It was like being plugged directly into the current of existence. Since then, the experience has returned only rarely during meditation, but I've found it can be triggered through music as well. Certain pieces act like tuning forks, aligning me in an instant to that same vivid, pulsing stillness. It's not something I can chase. When I try, it slips away. But when I'm fully present, it can just arise. Yet, as profound as these moments are, they come with a subtle lesson about attachment and impermanence.

Many who experience this might mistake it for the end goal, but in the Buddhist tradition, even these states of bliss, pīti, or rapture, are considered distractions on the path. They are signposts, not destinations. The instruction is to notice, acknowledge, and keep moving. Letting go even of the divine, even of the ecstasy, because grasping at it reinforces the very illusion of separation we're trying to transcend.

Still, the fact that such phenomena arise naturally hints at something profound. These arise unprompted and uninvited, yet they aren't hallucinations or wishful thinking. They are the body's deep intelligence responding to inner silence. They remind us that we don't need to add anything to become whole. All we ever needed was already inside, waiting for us to get quiet enough to feel it. This inner wholeness, once felt, reshapes how we carry our ego through the world, though not always in the same way.

Even when returning to this plane of understanding, the ego will not come back in the same way. After all, it died once, so there ought to be some things that are left on the other side, and there are some things we brought from there. In most cases, we probably return with greater compassion for the world, as the realization would mean that harming the world means harming ourselves. This might not be true for everybody, though. It highly depends on your previous journey, and for some people, the armor that they had to drop reassembles in a different manner. Some might conclude that they are God in the sense in which the Abrahamic god was described, a sole patriarch with everything there for them to take. Again, others will dismiss the entire experience as a construct of their subconscious, and in a sense, that is probably true as well. The only remaining conclusion is that there seems to be some sort of reproducible experience, which would make it something that could be scientifically researched.

There is no need to give it a label, however, as that is part of what makes this realization joyful. It is impossible to label most of the things you experience. Even my explanation is but a mere reference to the linear understanding we have. We can, however, deduce that there seems to be a substantial shift in how we walk through the world afterward. For most, this shift positively altered their reality. So it leaves beneficial effects on your day-to-day life. As these substances are not new on the face of the earth, we can assume that they have been used for centuries. This leads to a wild but potentially true thesis, like the „stoned ape theory." But with utmost certainty, mystics of their time must have encountered psychedelic substances, trying to explain their findings to their followers and leaving profound pearls of wisdom for people to live a better life.

Some of these mystics are probably known as today's religious figures, probably being peaceful rebels of their time. But our human understanding of nature only works within the constraints of time, body, and environment, which leads to people misunderstanding their teachings as they build groups to interpret what was said, creating one of the limitations I put quite the emphasis on to unleash the reader from. This group of people becomes a cult and eventually a religion, butchering the very ideal that the individual tried to share. These ancient insights, often lost in translation, inspired the journey this book seeks to share with you.

The purpose of this book was indeed to guide the reader to the eternal now. However, this is not the end of the journey; rather, it is the beginning. You have just transformed the most mundane activity into one of your most intense experiences. In the process, you might have realized that the quest for meaning never truly made sense, as you are already experiencing the meaning of life. This realization leaves you with a new challenge: discovering how intense an experience you can create in this life.

Surprisingly, I will not advocate the use of psychedelic substances to reach this state. While I did indeed use them, I don't think everyone is safe to use them, and it is, at this point, impossible to say who is safe using them. But probably even more importantly, you are meant to achieve this state naturally. They are a shortcut, giving you the temporary benefit of what you should incorporate into your life anyway. Depending on psychedelics means you are running the show from the wrong side, and as such, you might lose your act. But if you know that you can safely use them, then you could see them like training wheels on a bike. If you never learn to ride without your training wheels, you are not a cyclist, though. This natural path to clarity is built through deliberate practices, ones I've woven into my own life to uncover moments of profound presence.

I've laid out every step for a reason. It wasn't just about feeling better or surviving chaos. Tuning the body, sharpening attention, letting go of the noise: these practices had a deeper purpose. Moving daily didn't just build my lungs; it grounded me in the now, shaking off the stories my head spun about who I'd been. Eating real food wasn't a diet trick. It steadied the chemical storms, clearing the fog so I could hear the quiet underneath. Focusing my attention and cutting the Netflix marathons wasn't self-denial. It trained me to stop chasing shadows and sit with what's real. Each piece was a chisel, chipping at the illusions until one night, sprawled under a desert sky after months on the road, the world dropped away: no me, no past, just the hum of everything. Satori.

That sudden clarity isn't a trophy you earn. It's what emerges when the tools strip back the clutter. Picture a lens smeared with grime: it's not about building a new one, but wiping it clean. By moving your body, feeding it right, and focusing your mind, you wipe away the grime until the world sharpens into view. Isabelle didn't just endure cancer; she laughed through the haze until it parted. For me, it was a quiet morning, years back, sitting with a cup of tea, when the chatter stopped. Not forced, just gone. And everything clicked: simple, alive, unguarded. That glimpse didn't come from the road; it sent me there, a spark that turned chaos into a path. Satori isn't in the wiping; it's the clear sight you get when the grime's gone.

You don't need my exact path. Your dials are yours to tweak. Maybe it's a run that jolts you present, a meal that quiets the buzz, a moment staring at a tree until your thoughts shut up. The point isn't the how-to; it's the why: every small act tunes you closer to that unfiltered now. It's not a finish line. You might glimpse it today and lose it tomorrow. But once you've felt it, you know it's there, waiting behind the noise. That's the journey: not to chase

Satori, but to clear the way so it finds you. For me, this journey has crystallized into a simple yet profound choice to embrace life fully.

And so I choose to live, not because it's noble or grand, but because it's absurdly, messily mine. Want to know life's meaning? Step into it. Fall, laugh, get up. That's enough. This embrace of life's absurdity opens the door to a deeper state of presence, where true freedom resides.

Once you are fully comfortable sitting with yourself, without distractions, you are finally fully free. In this state, you'll experience profound bliss and unconditional love. An intensity unmatched by anything external. You will feel no need to identify yourself with anything anymore, and yet still know who you are. You are neither your job nor your free-time activities, nor any other groups you previously identified with. There is just this constant surge of love, abundance, and happiness going through you. By trying to hold onto it, it will vanish. As it is the very definition of freedom, holding onto it would mean it is not free anymore. Achieving this state of freedom begins with meditation, a practice that often reveals the mind's inner chaos before unveiling its clarity.

When you sit down to meditate, don't be surprised by the chaos arising. We have this picture of a monk peacefully sitting in the lotus pose for hours at a time, but it took him a long time to get there. If you experience intense chaos, it means you are doing everything right. The ancient tech-savvy folks among us might still remember that for your computer to function at its best, we needed to defragment the hard disc. The data printed on your hard drive was not printed in order, but wherever there was space left. The defragmentation was ordering the used storage, making the computer more efficient. When you sit down, your brain starts exactly this ordering process.

The first information that comes in is all the information that still has an emotional charge. This is the perfect opportunity to let go of the emotional baggage of this day or maybe even for years. Instead of reacting to it and falling victim to your mind dissecting the event, you can just observe it. This will create a distance between the experience and you, loosening any emotional charge still left on the experience. Remember that our usual helper, the ego, is not the best at defragmenting our hard drive. Whenever it arises, kindly guide it to the passenger seat. You do this by guiding it to a single thought. This can be a mantra, your breath, a memory of an object, or a point in your body. It is easier to drop a single thought than a thousand thoughts. When the mind is finally focused on a singular point, you let it go.

You have arrived!